STOLE PATTERNS

STOLE PATTERNS

Counted Cross Stitch

Jeff Wedge

MOREHOUSE-BARLOW

Wilton, Conn.

The line drawings in this book were drawn by
Scott Collins and Nancy Lou Makris.

Morehouse-Barlow Co., Inc.
78 Danbury Road
Wilton, Connecticut 06897

Library of Congress Cataloging-in-Publication Data

Wedge, Jeff.
Stole patterns.

Includes index.
1. Cross stitch—Patterns. 2. Ecclesiastical
embroidery. 3. Stoles (Clothing) 4. Church vestments.
I. Title.
TT771.W446 1986   746.9'2   85-61216
ISBN 0-8192-1398-5

Printed in the United States of America

2 4 6 8 10 9 7 5 3 1

To two sisters,
the one who taught me to cross stitch,
and the one who taught me more,
this book is lovingly dedicated.

CONTENTS

STOLE PATTERNS

THE STOLE

Jesus said, "Come to me, all of you who are tired from carrying heavy loads, and I will give you rest. Take my yoke and put it on you, and learn from me, because I am gentle and humble in spirit; and you will find rest. For the yoke I will give you is easy, and the load I will put on you is light."   Matthew 11:28–30 (TEV)

The stole, the particular garment which signifies the ordained ministry, is often presented as a symbolic representation of these words of Jesus. The precise origins and meanings of the garment are not quite this simple.

One early use of stoles was by deacons who served at tables. The stole worn by deacons was, and is, somewhat different from the stole worn by the ordained clergy, but the connection with a meal is significant. The stole is still worn by those who serve at the meal of the Lord, the Eucharist, whether clergy or deacon.

Another traditional origin for the stole insists that the garment comes from the napkin which was worn at meals to brush away crumbs and insects. This napkin was worn around the neck much as stoles are today.

The first generalized use of the stole as the distinctive garment for ordained clergy was in the Eastern Church. By the seventh century this use had spread through much of the Church, but often the form and color of the stole varied widely.

As a symbol of the yoke of Christ the stole is often ornamented with a cross or other symbol of Christ. The use of symbols is, in some circles, controversial. There are those who hold that the stole should be plain and unornamented. Although there are some good points in this argument, one simple fact needs to be acknowledged. The stole, with appropriate symbols, can be an excellent tool for teaching and enhancing the faith of the people who see it.

Today stoles are most often worn around the neck and hung from the shoulders, down the chest of the wearer. Often, especially when celebrating the Eucharist, the stole, worn over the alb or surplice, is crossed over the chest. It usually matches the color of the other paraments in the church, the color appointed in the liturgical calendar for the season or event which is being celebrated.

The symbols used on a stole should be symbols appropriate to the season or day on which the stole is worn. If particular symbols for a given day seem a little beyond your capacities at this time, then a general symbol such as a cross should probably be used on all the stoles of a set. However, it should be obvious that the symbols which are most appropriate for Christmas would be much less appropriate for the Easter Season, even though white is the color appointed for both times.

With almost two thousand years of experience and usage one might expect that there should be some sort of universal agreement about the meanings of the symbols we use. Generally there is not. In fact, there is not always agreement about what symbol should be known by a particular name. For example, each of the crosses in Figure 1 is called, in a different reference, a Jerusalem cross.

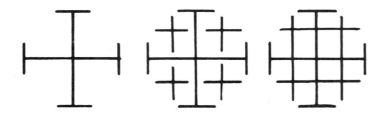

Fig. 1. Jerusalem crosses.

Perhaps this lack of absolute agreement about the name and meaning of each symbol should not be taken as a serious problem. Symbols mean something slightly different to each person who sees them. The absence of a strictly defined meaning should be taken as a sign that the Christian Church, taken as a whole, is still a growing, changing entity. This is certainly a sign of the basic health of the Church, but it is also a frustration to someone trying to explain what these symbols mean.

The stole itself is often taken as a symbol of the yoke of Christ. But it is also related to the office of the deacon and those who serve at the table of the Lord. Further, it is also presented, at different times, as a sign of patience, as a reminder of the robe of new life that Christ has won for us, or as a sign of the innocence of our first parents. The garment embodies at least these meanings and perhaps even other, more personal meanings as well.

The explanations of the symbols which follow are, to the best of my knowledge, all within the body of Christian tradition. They are not meant as exhaustive explanations and they are certainly somewhat personal. They are not intended to exclude other meanings or interpretations. They are simply offered to help you decide on the symbols you prefer to use on the stoles you make.

There are many styles of stoles which traditionally have been used. One style has been labeled "Byzantine." This style of stole is distinguished by its uniform width and by the use of a keeper chain to keep the fabric of the stole off the neck of the wearer.

All of the stoles in this book of patterns are intended to be of the Byzantine style. This type of stole is appropriate for use with the alb style of vestment because it is generally longer and wider than other stoles and, thus, most suitable for the longer lines of the alb. These stoles are not difficult to construct. In addition, they have the advantage of being quite long-lasting because they are not discolored by moisture from the neck of the wearer.

TAILORING STOLES

Even though many ready-made stoles are only available in a single size, the people who wear them are available in many sizes. Since you are going to be making stoles with a particular person in mind, you will be able to make stoles that are exactly right. The dimensions and patterns given for stoles in this book are intended to be a springboard for you to use in creating your own stoles.

There is no rule which states that the *only* correct way for the symbols charted in this book to be placed on a stole is the way they are placed on the samples. Any of the locations in Figure 2 would be appropriate, or almost any other pattern you find should work as well.

The dimensions of a particular stole may be adapted to suit more closely the individual who will be wearing it. One clergy couple has two sets of stoles: One set is shorter and narrower than average, the other is longer and wider, to suit the physical differences between a petite wife and a tall husband.

The dimensions and placement of patterns suggested in this book will result in a completely adequate set of stoles. You are invited, however, to modify the dimensions and locations of the designs as you desire. It might be helpful to give you a formula for modifying the dimensions given here to suit your size so you could figure out how much material you need for a stole. Instead, let me offer a *number* and a *suggestion*. The number is two, as in two yards of material. If you are very tall, then get a little more; otherwise two yards of material should suffice for a stole. Actually, most people will be able to make two stoles from one piece of material two yards long. The suggestion is, fit it the way I do. Cut a sample using the measurements given in the next chapter from an old sheet or paper bags taped together. Try it on and make any changes needed to suit your taste. Remember to allow at least an inch of extra material for seams and hems. And be sure to write down the dimensions you finally decide on, since you will want them later when you start on the second stole.

To some extent, the colors listed for both the material and the thread, called *floss*, in this book are meant as suggestions. If you prefer using a different color, you are free to use it. Many of the designs have suggestions in the text accompanying them

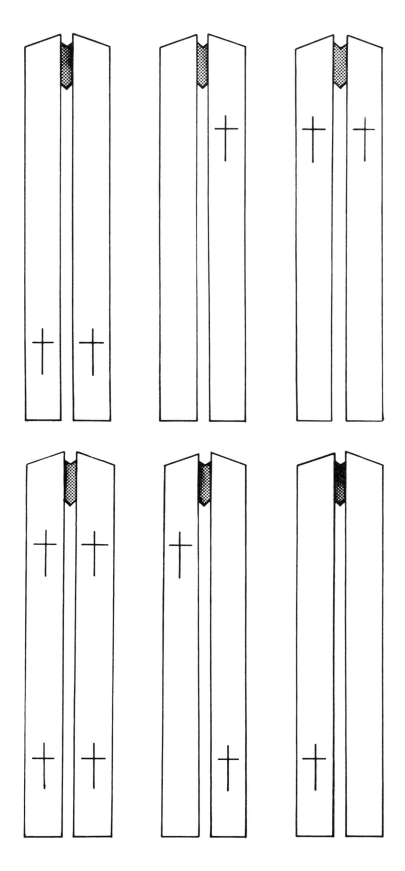

Fig. 2. Possible locations for symbols or crosses on stoles.

for modifications and other uses, but additional modifications are certainly possible. For instance, a particular cross could be used on all the stoles of a set to make that set uniform.

Selecting the Material

Making stoles, like any form of craftsmanship, is a personal thing. It would be presumptuous of me to dictate exactly how you should go about every little detail. I have preferences, but you might prefer doing things another way. As long as the completed stole is acceptable to the person who will be wearing it, either your way or my way is fine. There are, however, some suggestions I would like to offer for making the stoles in this book.

About the material to use for making a stole: all the samples for this book have been worked on burlap. Burlap offers many advantages for making stoles. It is readily available, usually in a wide variety of colors. The only real problem I have had is finding two shades of red so I can use one as the scarlet stole for Holy Week. Both blue and purple are available, but some places may have to order the material for you. To be sure, some colors will rub off on the robe, but it washes right out of the alb. Burlap is one of the least expensive fabrics available, a fact that keeps down the cost of the stole and allows a little extra for practice. And, finally, burlap offers a certain rough texture for the finished stole that is an attractive complement to the alb.

Occasionally people seem to have a problem getting the stitches to come out correctly on the first try with burlap. This seems to resolve itself with practice (and is usually a matter of holding the floss either too tightly or too loosely), and the practice is worth it.

Burlap is not a perfectly even-weave fabric, and the major disadvantage of burlap is that it can be quite irregular. This may be an insurmountable problem for you. If it is, the patterns will work on an even-weave cloth such as Aida 11 (that means 11 squares to the inch). The designs will be a little smaller, the cost of each stole will be greater, and you may have some problem finding Aida cloth in pieces that are two yards long, but it can be done. Aida cloth comes in a variety of colors, so you may not need to dye the material to get the colors you need.

I want to encourage you to seriously consider burlap as the material to use when you are making a stole, although some people are allergic to the substances used to make or dye burlap. If you are allergic, then please use something else as the material for your stole. If burlap or Aida is out of the question, you might wish to consider still another possibility. Fair warning, however, because this possibility promises to be the most expensive and most complicated of the choices. It is possible to do counted cross stitch on any material, even silk or satin, if you wish. After you have prepared the material by following the directions in the next chapter, but before you start on the design, attach (with pins, or with basting stitches) a piece of Aida cloth (or some other even-weave material) to the place where the design is going to be. The next is the tricky part. You *must* get the Aida perfectly straight, which is not easy on a material like silk or satin. Then, stitch the design, using the Aida cloth to keep your stitches even. When you are done, use tweezers to pull out the Aida cloth, thread by thread. If the threads stick within the design, try getting them damp; sometimes that will loosen them up.

To use the method of Aida cloth on other material, you will need a piece of Aida cloth that is a little larger than the pattern you will be working. Each of the patterns in this book includes the dimensions of the pattern. Simply divide the dimensions of the pattern by the number of the Aida cloth you are using, round off upward, and add a half-inch or so to allow for a small margin. For example, Design 9 is 55 stitches wide by 72 high. You should have a piece of Aida 11 that is about 5½ by 7 inches (55 divided by 11 equals 5 plus ½ inch is 5½ inches wide; 72 divided by 11 equals 6½ plus ½ inch is 7 inches high).

Like all the patterns in the book, I have tried working cross stitch on satin. All of the suggestions here are based on my experience. And if you decide to use this method to make a stole from silk or satin, let me point out that it will be more expensive than using burlap or even Aida cloth. Also, be very careful to get things straight in the beginning, otherwise you may discover that you have spent quite a few hours putting a design that is crooked on the stole. I have sometimes fixed mistakes, but that is a mistake I don't even like to think about.

Using the Designs

The next group of suggestions are about the patterns in this book. As you look through this volume, don't give up immediately on a pattern that does not look like much. It might help to get a set of colored pencils, preferably pencils that you can erase (in case you slip, as I have discovered I sometimes do). Use the pencils to color in the pattern in the book. Color it lightly so you can still see all the details. This will help you discover what the pattern contains. You might find that you like it, and when it comes to the actual working of the pattern, the colors will help.

At times the hobby of counted cross stitch has a less than reputable side. This involves the use of a copying machine to reproduce the designs for other people who do not buy the book. Such a practice is, of course, reprehensible, and you will certainly never engage in it. But there are at least two times when you might wish to make a copy of a pattern for your own use. These times are neither reprehensible nor improper.

First, there are some designs in this book which are simply too large to fit on a single page. They might be easier to execute if you get a copy made of all the pages with part of the design and then, with scissors and tape, make yourself a one-page pattern to work from.

Second, you might wish to modify a design. Design 17 is followed by two examples of how that design might be modified. Suggestions also are made at other points in the book for modifying other designs. If you find that you need or want to modify any of the designs, you are welcome to do so. I would suggest a copy of the original for making modifications. This is also a place to use your colored pencils.

Floss

Finally, some suggestions about the floss. When you go out to buy the floss for the design you have chosen, there are a couple of suggestions I would offer. Buy lots of floss for the first stole. After that, you will be better able to judge how much floss you are likely to need for a pattern. There is a chart at the end of the book which details the colors used in each design. Any floss left over from the first design will be useable for another one later. So, the second suggestion is like the first: buy LOTS of floss.

If you are anything like me, you will be astonished at the way the floss seems to melt away as you are using it. I have very long arms and am able to use a full skein of floss without cutting it. Even with that advantage (and each time you cut the skein you are giving up at least six inches of floss) a stole made with designs 7 and 8 required parts of eighteen skeins of floss. You should expect to use many skeins of floss. Don't be afraid of that, but DO be sure to buy enough floss to finish a design. Stores sometimes change the brand of floss they carry, and not all colors are available in every brand. Sometimes the same color in two different brands is not exactly the same color. I would offer a final rule of thumb to help: If in doubt, buy another skein.

Not too surprisingly, the largest part of the cost of the stoles I have made has been the floss. In general, it is probably better to have extra floss than it is to run out of floss at an hour when the stores are closed with only a few stitches left to finish a pattern. By now you might have noticed that the cost of the stole is a large part of my concern, so let me end this chapter on an economic note about floss.

I usually buy the large amounts of floss I need at a local discount store. The house brand floss usually costs about half of what a national brand costs. In addition, the national brands have only 8.7 yards of floss in a skein, while the discount store skeins usually have 9 yards.

The less expensive floss does not have quite the sheen of the national brands, but since these stoles are meant to be seen at a distance, the difference really doesn't matter. One thing should be pointed out: If you will be working on silk or satin, you might want to consider using the national brands. In this special case the extra sheen is better.

All of this brings up the matter of what you might expect a stole to cost. I will not give a specific answer. The cost depends on many variables, but I will point out that the most expensive stole I have made cost less than ten dollars for materials. The more stoles you make, the lower your average cost per stole will be. When you start making the second stole in a particular color, you will be able to use the other half of the two yards of material you bought for the first stole, and your cost will drop even lower. To put it another way, including the cost of this book and a reasonable figure for the cost of materials, you should be able to make at least a dozen stoles for yourself—possibly as many as two dozen—for the cost of four ready-made stoles.

ASSEMBLING THE STOLE

The following directions lead to the construction of a Byzantine style stole. A byzantine stole, regardless of the connotations of the word "Byzantine," is the simplest style to make since it involves only straight seams and hems. The dimensions included in these directions lead to a standard size stole. If desired, these dimensions may be modified to fit a particular person. Patterns for other styles of stoles are available, along with charts for further designs, in a book by Rev. William R. Doser titled *Clergy Stoles*. In addition, any cross stitch design that will fit on a stole may be used.

In the previous chapter the possibility of using a material other than an even-weave fabric was discussed. Please check those directions if you are using such material for your stole.

Although the whole idea of this book is to use counted cross stitch to make the designs on the stole, it is possible to use the designs as patterns for another fabric such as felt; cut it out and sew the felt onto the stole. If you are doing that, simply skip past the part that explains how to do cross stitch.

1. Select the appropriately colored material (or dye a piece of material to the appropriate color and let it dry throughly). Considering the amount of effort that is going into the construction of the stole, scrimping on the quality of the basic fabric is not a good idea. Be sure that the fabric is an even-weave material suitable for cross stitch work (with the exceptions noted in the paragraph above). Cut two pieces of material 10 inches wide and 62 inches long. Or, cut the two yards of material in half (the long way). Put one half aside for the second stole in this color, and cut the other half in half again (also the long way). Check Figure 3 for an idea of the shape of the pieces you will end up with.

Use masking tape (or a rough zig-zag stitch) to tape all the edges that might fray. It is also possible to use a commercial preparation to prevent fraying. Some of these preparations have names such as Frayguard, Stopfray, and Fray-No-More. Be sure to use a small piece of your material to experiment with first, since these preparations may stain the material. The object here is to keep the material from fraying too much while you are working on it.

2. Apply the designs to the face of the stole. Two things must be noted about this step. "Apply" means to put the designs on the stole. If you are using counted cross stitch, that is the method of applying the designs. If you are simply using some other material for the designs, then attach it. Be very careful to get the designs in the proper position on the material, as illustrated in Figure 3. Obviously, Figure 3 involves four designs. If you are using less than four designs, place them accordingly. It is the position on the fabric that is important, not the number of designs. Be sure

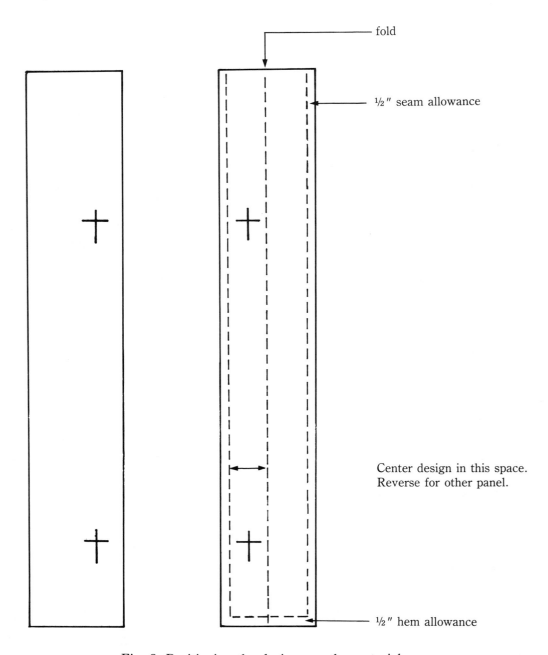

Fig. 3. Positioning the designs on the material.

to allow at least a half-inch on each side of the panel for the seam (if you have a panel ten inches wide, then the finished stole, allowing for the seam, will be 4½ inches wide).

3. To turn the patterns in this book into symbols on a stole, you must work one cross stitch for each square on a particular chart. The following steps deal with the way to do cross stitch.

a. Wash your hands. Then, pretend that you are five years old again and hold out your hands for your mother to inspect. Go wash them again. (At least that is what my mother usually said!) There is a reason for this insistence on clean hands. I have no idea what will happen to the burlap if you wash it, but the thought does make me nervous. In addition, because of government regulations, not all the colors of floss are color-fast as they come from the store. Some of the colors of floss and likely some colors of burlap will loose their color (or even worse, the colors will run onto the nearby material and ruin the stole) if you have to wash the stole. Save yourself the trouble. Go wash your hands again.

b. Now get comfortable. Take a good look at the pattern and spend a little while planning how you intend to work the design (where will you start, which color should you do first, where will the symbol be on the finished stole, and so on).

c. Thread your needle (a tapestry needle, size 22, works very well with burlap) with a suitable length of floss. You will have to decide what a suitable length is. I would suggest that it should be at least 24 inches, probably longer. When you are deciding how long the floss should be, remember, longer pieces tend to get tangled more often. Shorter pieces mean that you will be stopping and starting more often, and you will be using the floss more rapidly.

d. Find the center of the pattern (marked by the arrows on the edge of each pattern) and count out the distance to the first stitch. Then find the center of the location for the design on the material, and count out to the proper place for the first stitch (don't forget to allow for the hem).

e. Two ways to work stitches are shown in Figure 4. Be sure to leave a short tail behind your first stitch so that you can catch it on the back of the piece with the next few stitches.

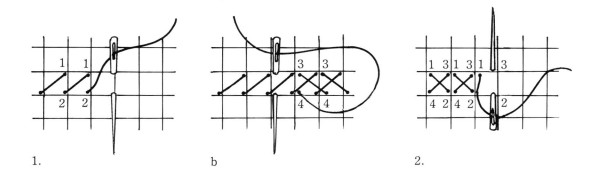

Fig. 4. Two ways to work cross stitch. The second method uses more floss.

It is recommended that you work with all six strands of floss when cross stitching on burlap. (If that sentence confused you, don't worry. Floss as it comes from the store is composed of six strands.) Design 17 requires a different stitch that is illustrated at that point. Design 22 is the only design in this book that should be stitched with less than six strands. The directions at that place tell you what to do.

You may wish to experiment to achieve the look you desire. It is possible to use fewer than six strands to work a pattern. The fewer strands you use, the more closely the pattern will follow the basic irregularities of the burlap. Or, put another way, fewer strands will produce a design that is slightly more open, slightly less crowded. If you wish to experiment, try a simple pattern (such as a small square) on a piece of scrap material with 3 or 4 strands. Using fewer strands will, of course, help the floss go farther.

f. Keep stitching until you come to the end of the stitches in this color. When the last stitch is completed, turn the material over and finish off the color by running the floss under a few stitches. If you run out of floss before you complete the color, simply finish off the piece of floss and continue with more floss.

g. Now that you know how to do counted cross stitch, let me offer some suggestions from my own experience (and from the experience of some friends who run cross stitch supply stores).

You do not have to impress anyone by memorizing the pattern. It is in the book to help you. Consult it regularly, and do not trust your memory. More than once I was sure that the row was supposed to have 23 stitches, when the pattern distinctly showed only 21. Don't be proud, count it again, and you won't have to spend hours ripping out half of your work.

Don't "carry" the floss more than two stitches from where you are if at all possible. Cross stitch that is excellently done will always have a neat looking reverse side. In fact, when I go into a cross stitch store to brag about a finished piece, the people who work in the store usually don't say much until they look at the back of the piece.

You might wish to work with a hoop. I never have, but many people find that a hoop makes the work easier. Using a stretching frame or hoop is fine (anything that makes it easier is fine), but please be aware of the possible dangers. Hoops can leave circles impressed on the finished piece. So, if you do use a hoop, always take it off the material when you finish working for the day. Certainly, you are planning to go back to work on the stole the next day. I always mean to get back to the piece I am working on the next day as well. And I remind myself of those good intentions when I finally get around to resuming work a week (or a month) later.

Never leave your needle in the material. Never ever. When you are finished working for the moment, just fold up the material with the needle inside the material, but never jab the needle through the material. Not only does this sometimes cause a distortion in the material, a needle that has been used for a little while might very well have bare steel showing. Bare steel, and a few days, can very easily cause a rust spot that would ruin an otherwise perfect piece.

To finish the cross stitch instructions, and get back to making the stole, two notes. Keep your hands spotlessly clean. And, most important of all, Have Fun!

4. When you have finished all the symbols for a stole, carefully remove the masking tape from the material. Please be careful not to pull threads from the material along with the masking tape (One thread, maybe two, are all right, but you are going to need something to put a seam in, so be careful).

5. Place the faces of the panels together (so the finished designs are touching, if they are opposite each other), and join the top with a seam that covers half the width of the stole at a 45 degree angle. Trim the excess material close to the seam. (If you purchased something like Fray-No-More, you might want to strengthen the material close to the seam.) The result of this step is found in Figure 5. If you desire, a small cross may be applied to the back of the stole at this point. To do this, simply open up the material and apply the cross on the good side of the fabric, centered on the seam you have just made.

6. Join the other half of the back of the stole at a 45 degree angle. Trim. Hem the bottom. See Figure 6 for the results of this step.

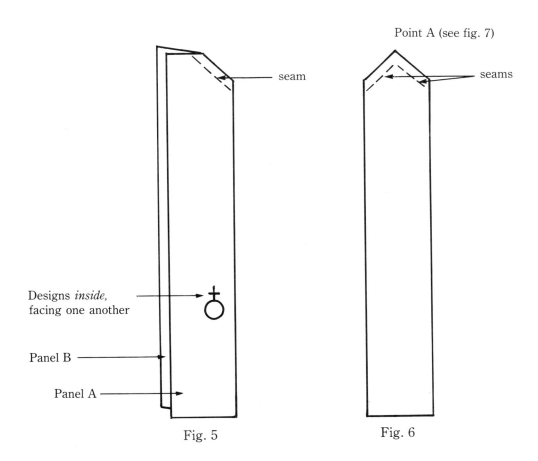

Point A (see fig. 7)

seam

seams

Designs *inside,* facing one another

Panel B

Panel A

Fig. 5

Fig. 6

7. Open the stole so that it will lie flat, inside out, with the two pieces meeting at a right angle. This is the position found in Figure 7. Join the long seams. Then, by passing the stole through itself, turn it right side out. The beginning of this process is also shown in Figure 7.

Add a six-inch-long chain at a point six inches from the joining seam on each of the inside edges of the stole. The keeper chain you have just added rides on the neck of the wearer so that the stole itself does not touch the neck.

8. Press the stole. It is now ready to be worn.

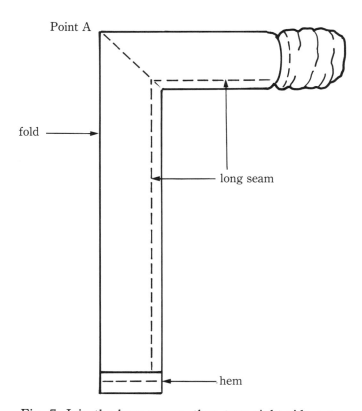

Fig. 7. Join the long seams, then turn right side out.

In closing, it should probably be pointed out that there is a long and venerable tradition of making liturgical garments locally. You are about to join that tradition (or you are about to begin a new dimension of your experience in that tradition). In some very important ways you will be working to spread the Word of God through your skill and artistry in constructing stoles.

STOLE DESIGNS

Design 1

CROSS WITH SUN'S RAYS BEHIND

Suggested for use in Advent or Easter

Dimensions: 54 stitches wide by 70 stitches high

Colors:

    ╱ = Gold
    ✗ = Red

The last chapter of the Old Testament, Malachi 4, includes many prophetic references to the "Day of the Lord." One of the images used here is the sun as a symbol of the power of the Lord. The image of power is appropriate for the season of Advent with its emphasis on preparation for the coming of the King. The prophecies of the Old Testament as the source for this image is also very appropriate for this season.

The use of rays of the sun behind a cross is also interpreted as a symbol of the glory of Christ. With this interpretation this design would be appropriate for the season (or day) of Easter. To use this design for a gold stole (for Easter Sunday), a border would probably have to surround the edge of the cross. If you wish to use this design in such a way, coloring the outer edge of the pattern or substituting another color for the gold (this would be the color of your choice) would probably be the best ways to modify this design.

Design 2

CROSS AND ORB

Suggested for use in Advent, Epiphany, or Pentecost

Dimensions: 52 stitches wide by 70 stitches high

Colors:

    ╱ = Gold
    ✕ = Red

The cross and orb symbol is considered to be a sign of the sovereignty of God over the world. This is the interpretation which is highlighted in the Advent season when we are reminded of the imminent arrival of the King. The orb is a representation of the world and is sometimes presented even more graphically as a globe.

Another interpretation says that this arrangement is a sign of the triumph of Christ over this world, and of Jesus's reign. Further, this is also taken as a sign of the triumph of the Gospel in the world. This last interpretation makes this an excellent design for use in the Epiphany season.

A variation of the last interpretation emphasizes the fact that the spread of the Gospel in the world is the mission of the Church. With this thought in mind, this symbol is also appropriate for the Pentecost season.

Design 3

"ICON" OF HERALDIC ANGEL

Suggested for use in Christmas

Dimensions: 56 stitches wide by 56 stitches high

Colors:

∕	=	Gold
6	=	Light Blue
3	=	Black
ɔ	=	White
∪	=	Flesh

The use of an angel during the Christmas season is obviously meant to be a reference to the various angels of the first two chapters of the Gospel of Luke. The English word "angel" comes directly from the Greek word *angelos* which means "messenger," an accurate description of the angel's function in Luke. The angel's hands are raised in benediction to emphasize this purpose and as a further reminder of the Gospel account. The cross over the angel's head is to remind us of the ultimate purpose of Christ's coming at Christmas.

This design and the three that follow are presented in two ways. The first pattern includes all the stitches of the design. The second page includes everything *except* the background. The third page has *only* the stitches of the background. This method of presenting the patterns should make them easier for you to follow.

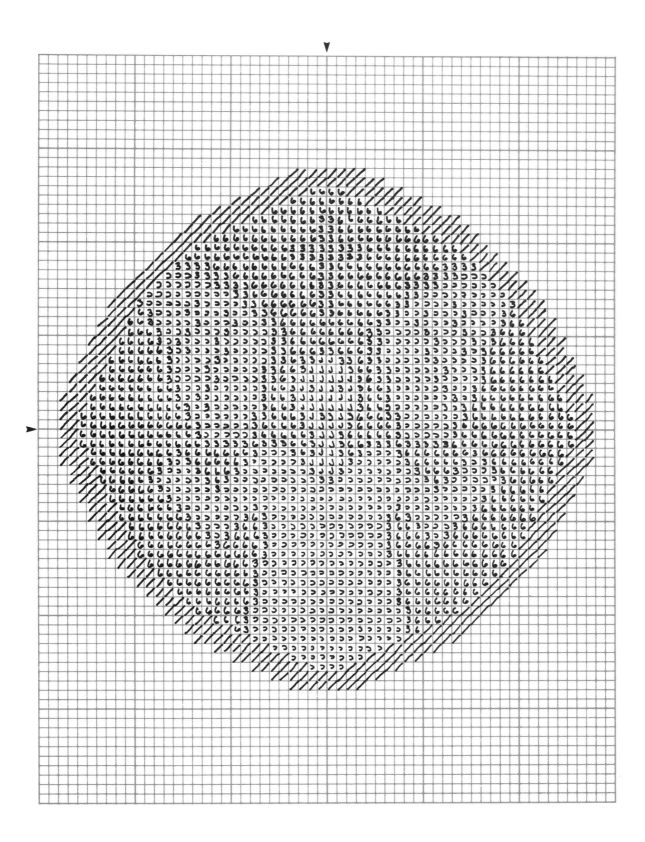

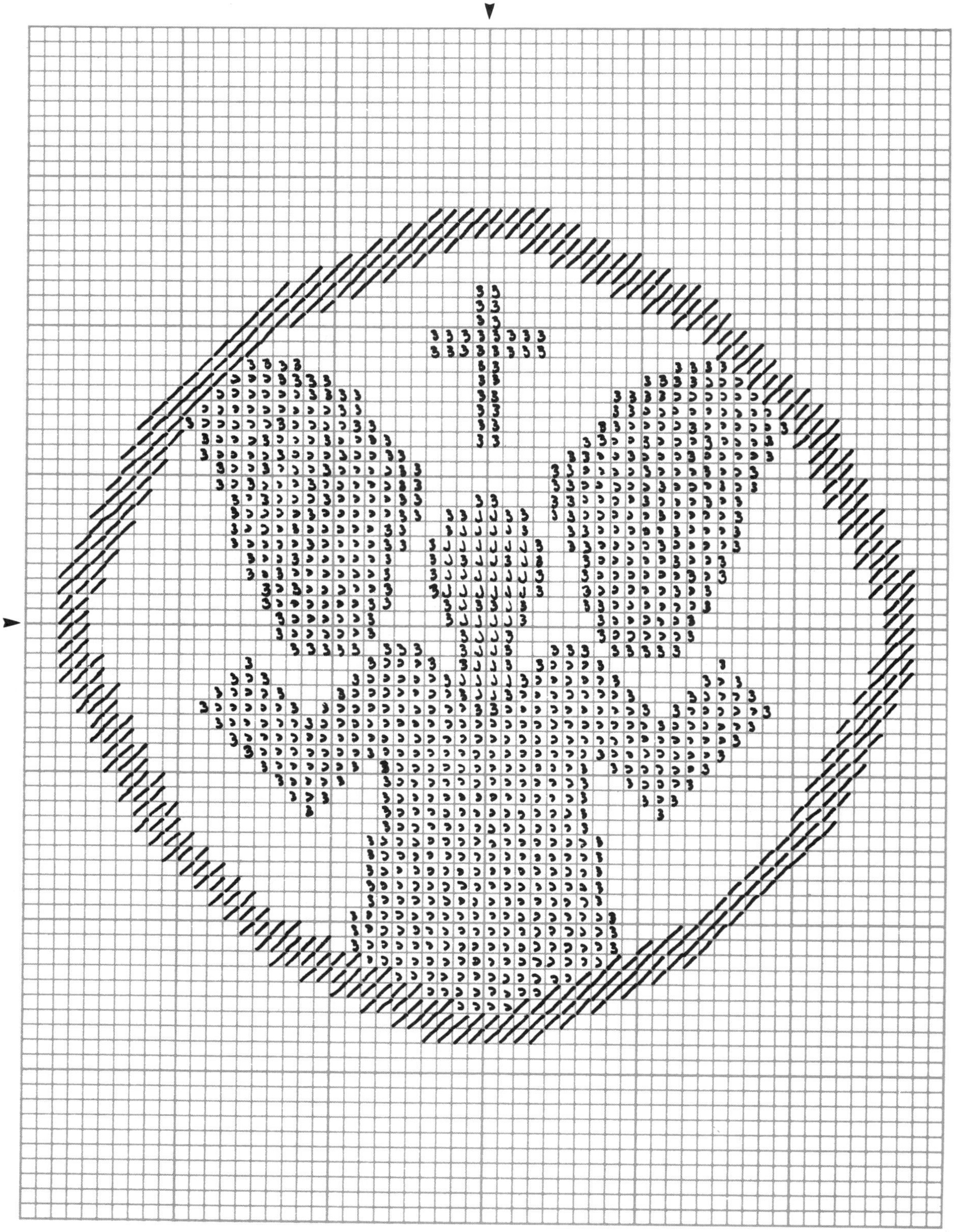

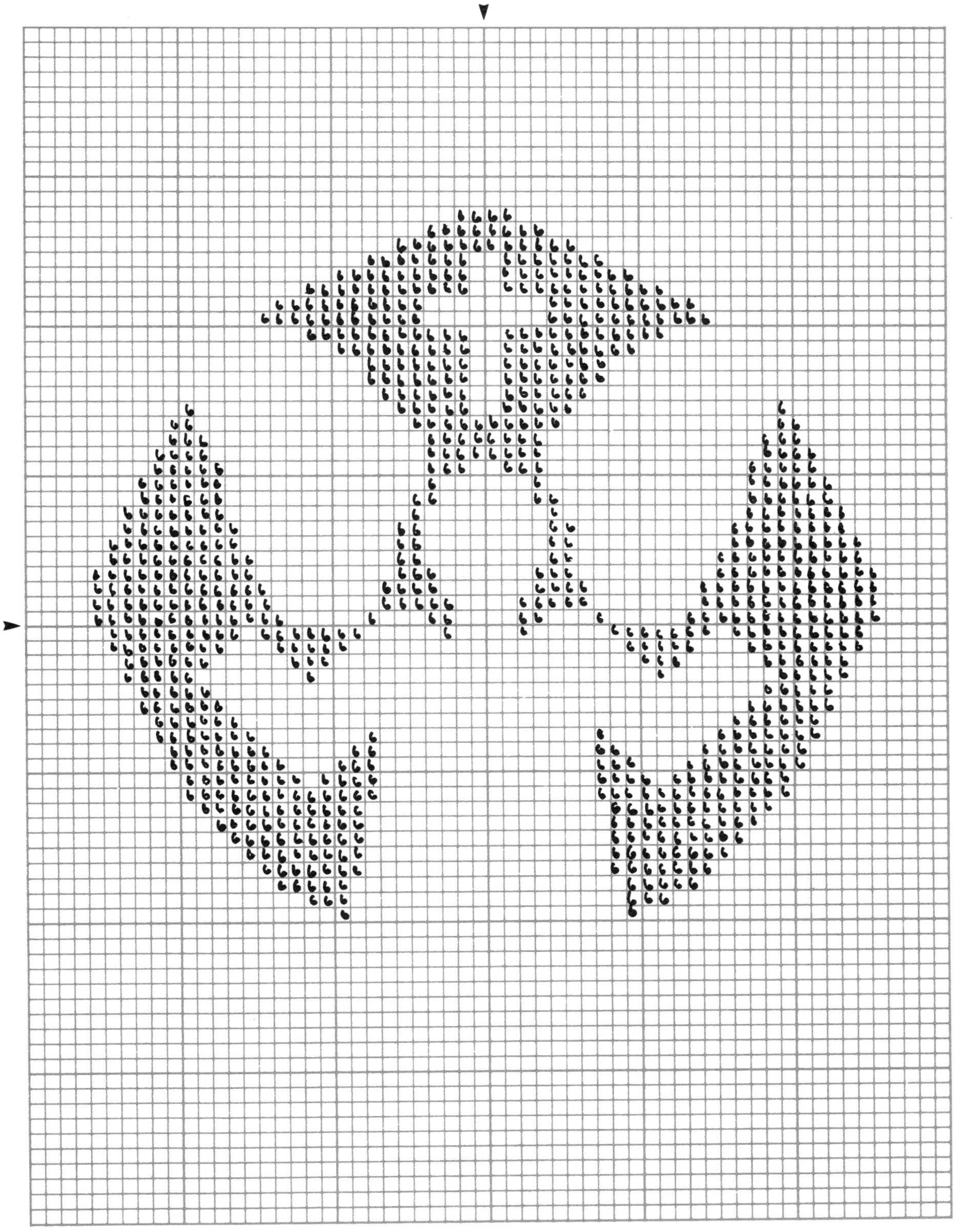

Design 4

"ICON" OF MANGER WITH IHC IN HALO

Suggested for use in Christmas

Dimensions: 56 stitches wide by 56 stitches high

Colors:

    ╱ = Gold
    6 = Light Blue
    Ɛ = Black
    Ɔ = White
    + = Medium Brown
    ✗ = Red

According to Luke 2:7, Jesus was laid in a manger. As a reminder of the humble setting of Jesus's birth, the manger is traditionally kept plain and simple. The halo surrounds a monogram which stands for the name of Jesus and is composed of the first three letters of the name in Greek. The final letter, "C," is a calligraphic variation of the Greek letter sigma (Σ).

The background color of the four iconic designs (3, 4, 5, and 6) is blue. This color is often associated with the Virgin Mary and is certainly appropriate for that reason alone during the Christmas season. Further, the color means, in heraldic usages, both heavenly love and the unveiling of the truth. These additional meanings make blue an appropriate background for both the Christmas and Epiphany seasons.

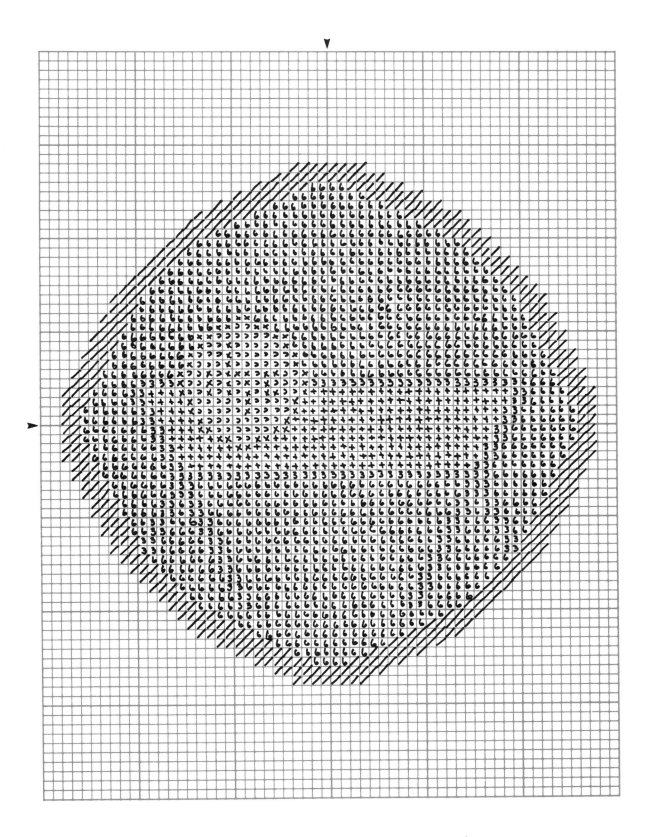

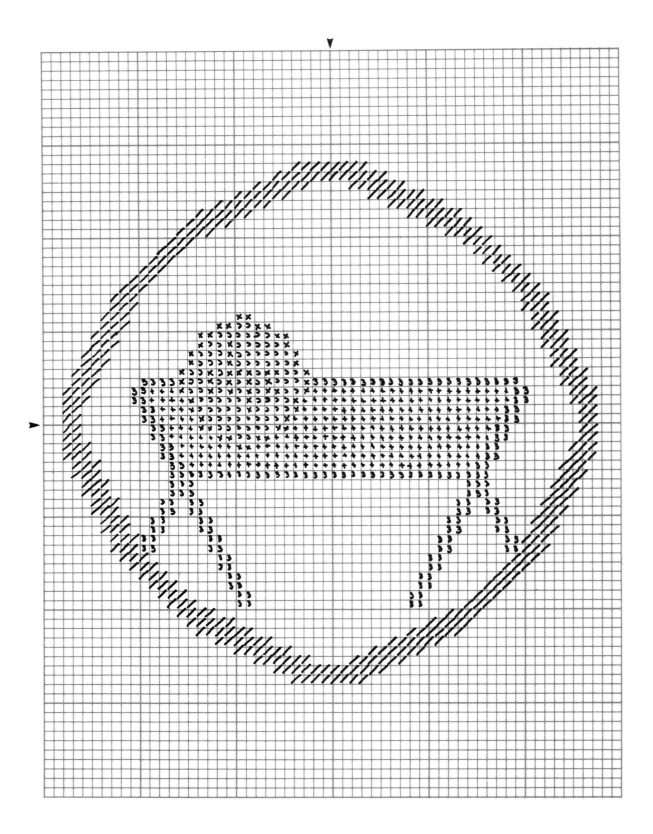

Design 5

"ICON" OF STAR

Suggested for use on the Day of the Epiphany

Dimensions: 55 stitches wide by 55 stitches high

Colors:

- ╱ = Gold
- ✔ = Light Blue
- 𝟑 = Black
- ᴐ = White

Sometimes the star is thought of as a symbol of the nativity, but this interpretation is contrary to the account of the Gospel according to Matthew. In that Gospel the Wise Men or Magi report in Jerusalem that they have seen a star which made known the birth of the King of the Jews.

January 6, the date of the Epiphany, is the traditional date given for the arrival in Bethlehem of the Magi and is the day when they are especially remembered. The day sets the tone for the season to follow with the star. The star *made known* the birth, and the season reminds us of the ways that God has made himself known to us.

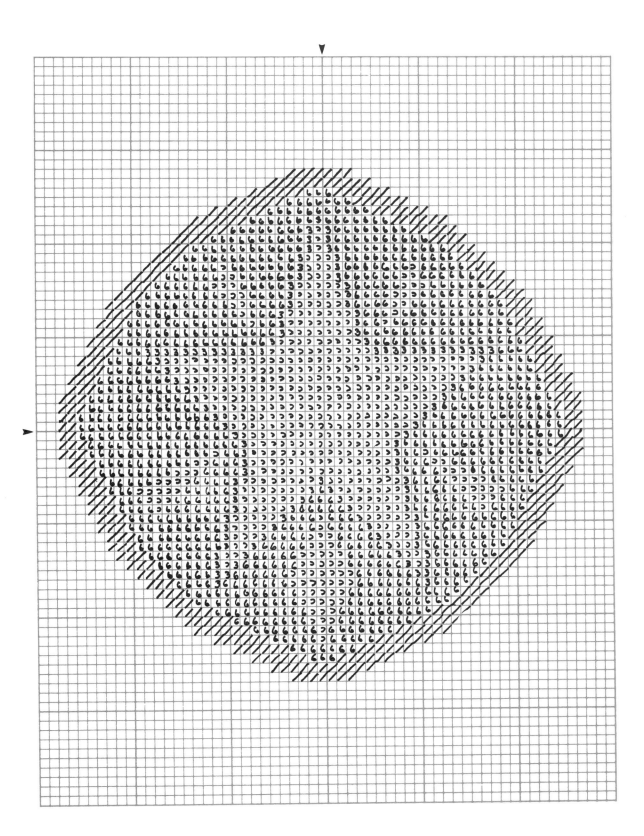

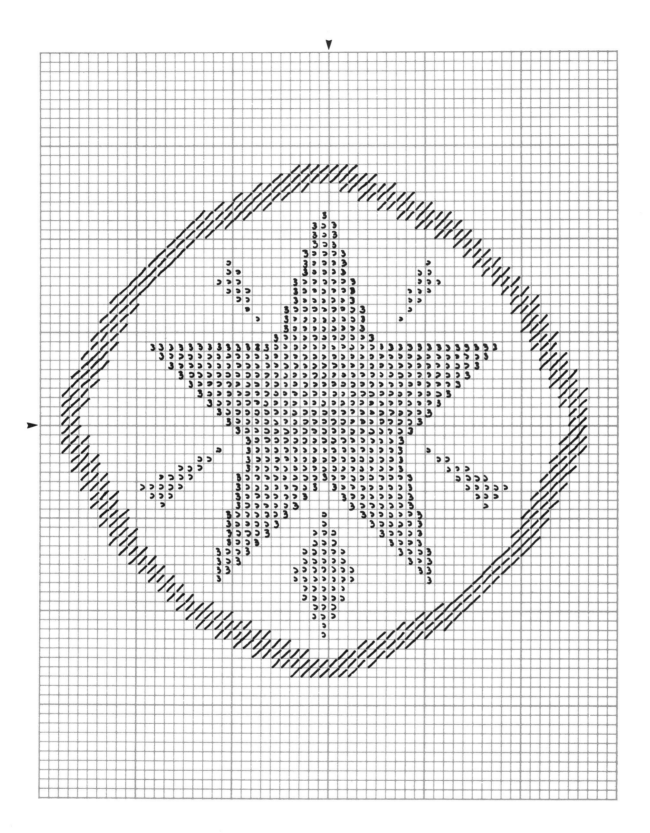

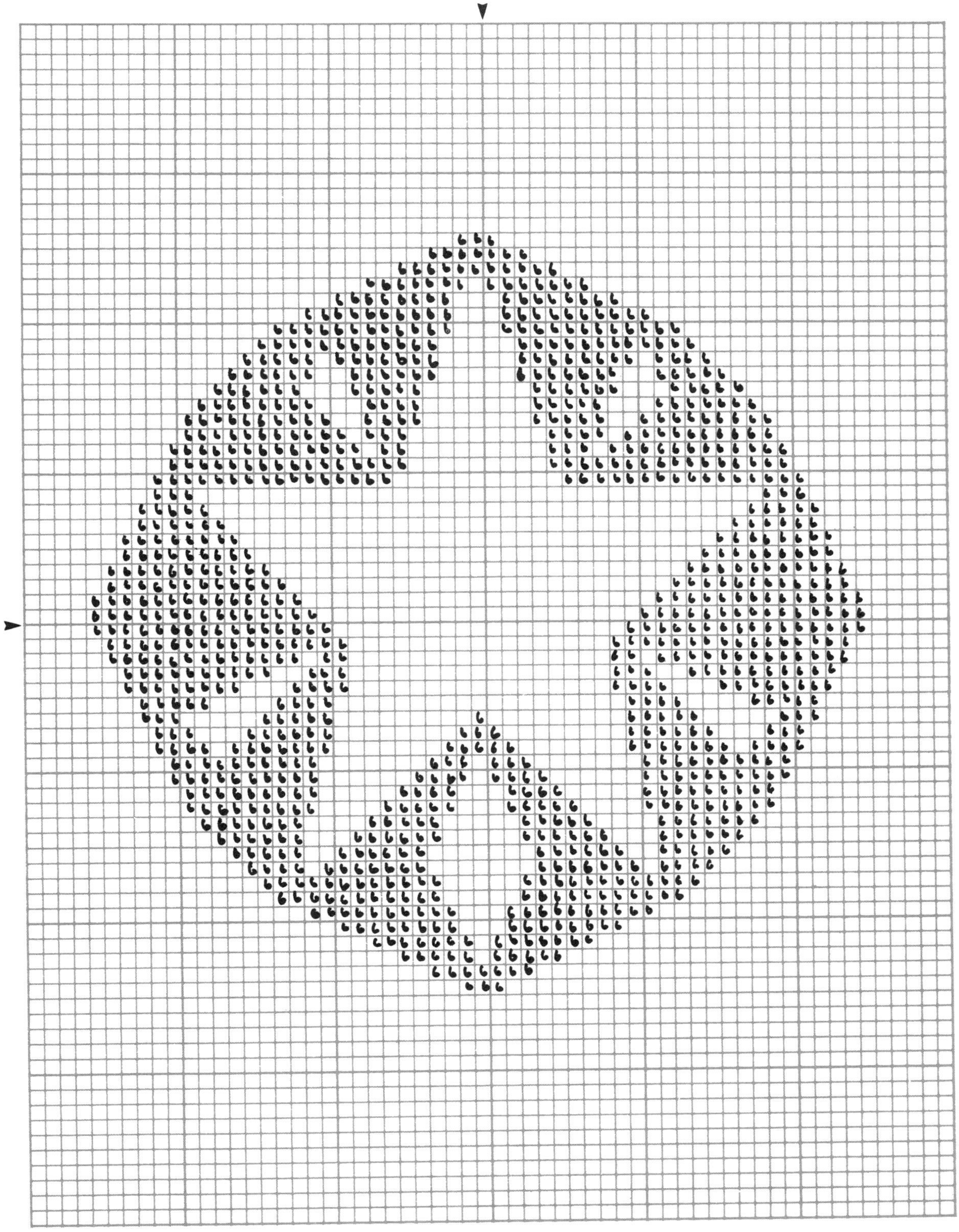

Design 6

"ICON" OF THREE CROWNS

Suggested for use on the Day of the Epiphany

Dimensions: 56 stitches wide by 56 stitches high

Colors:

/ = Gold
6 = Light Blue
3 = Black

The three crowns are a traditional symbol of the three mysterious Magi or Wise Men who came to Bethlehem to worship the Christ child. Based on the account of the visit in Matthew 2:1-18, the visit of the Magi may not have been quite what is often thought. In the first place, the Magi found the family at their house (Matthew 2:11). Judging from Herod's orders (Matthew 2:16), this visit might have been at any point up to the second birthday of Jesus.

Despite these alternative accounts, the Magi are closely related to the festival of the Epiphany. The name of the day and the season which follows means "to make known," especially in the sense of a manifestation or appearance of a god. The first time the Christ was worshipped was when the Magi came to visit. This worship is the first fulfillment of the prophecy of Simeon in Luke 2:32.

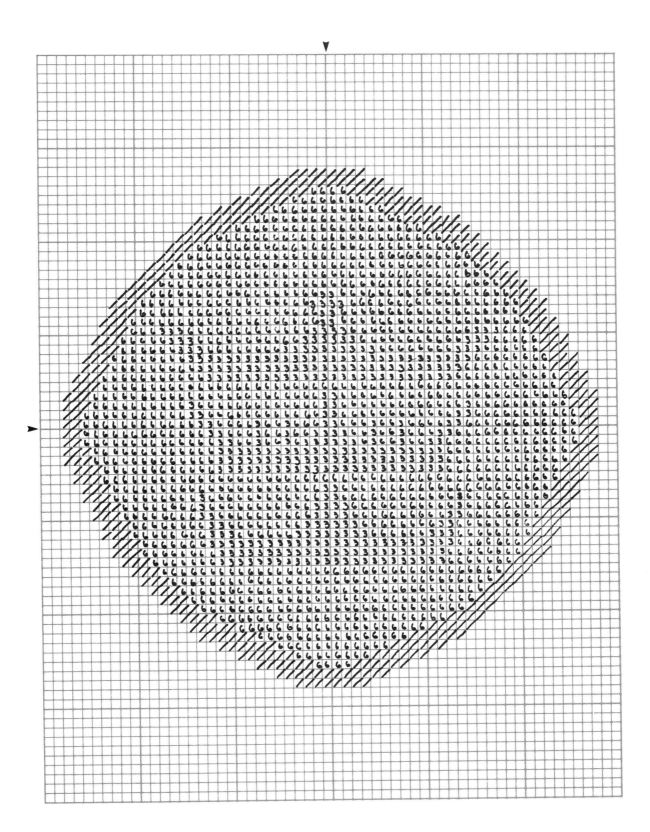

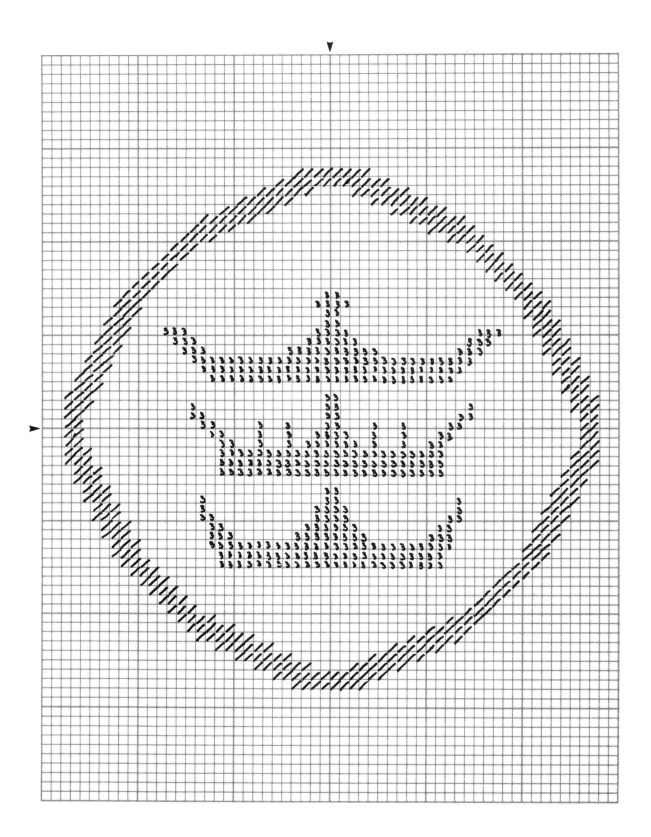

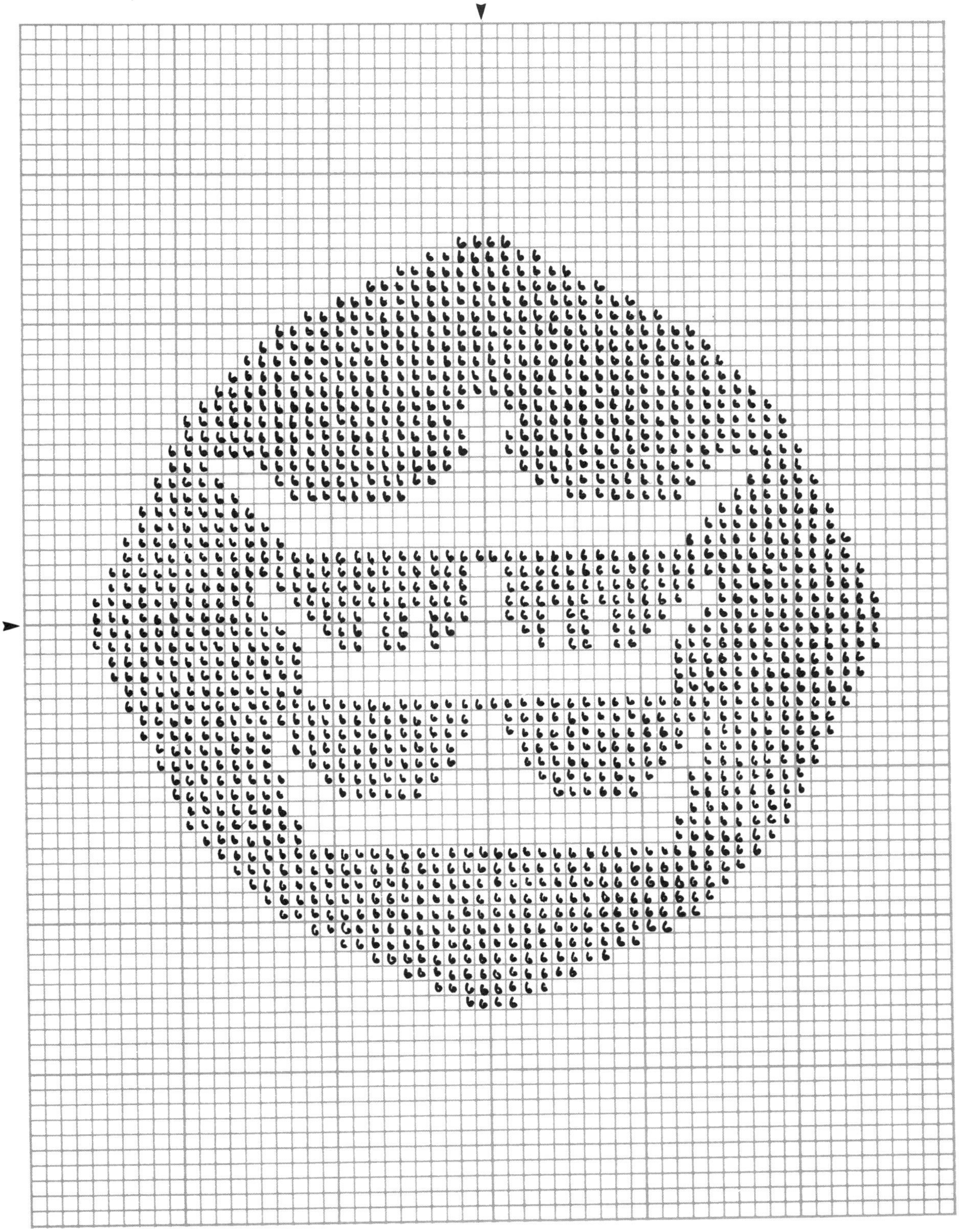

Design 7

CROSS-CROSSLET (JERUSALEM CROSS)

Suggested for use in Epiphany or Pentecost

Dimensions (excluding red stripes): 48 stitches wide by 94 stitches high

Colors:

- X = Red
- / = Gold
- S = Turquoise
- " = Pale Green
- ℈ = White

The cross-crosslet which is the basis for this design is sometimes called the Jerusalem Cross. The precise definition of which symbol should, most properly, be called the Jerusalem cross is not important for our purpose. What is important is that this is a symbol of the spread of the Gospel to the four corners of the world in fulfillment of the prophecy of Simeon at Jesus's circumcision (Luke 2:32). This design is, therefore, appropriate for either the season of Epiphany or the season of Pentecost.

It is possible to modify this design and the following design by eliminating the red stripes and white core and filling in the blank spaces with either gold or turquoise (or pale green), whichever is appropriate. If red stripes running the length of the stole appear a little daunting, it is also possible to extend the stripes for only a limited distance beyond the design.

Design 8

JERUSALEM CROSS (CANTONEE CROSS)

Suggested for use in Epiphany, Lent, or Pentecost

Dimensions (excluding red stripes): 48 stitches wide by 94 stitches high

Note: The red stripes run the length of the stole.

Colors:

- ✗ = Red
- ╱ = Gold
- ς = Turquoise
- ‖ = Pale Green
- ɔ = White

This design has much in common with the preceding design. Although both of these designs have been called the Jerusalem Cross, this form is more often thought of as the Jerusalem Cross. The basic meaning of the symbol, spreading the Gospel to the four corners of the earth, is the same for both versions. In addition, this design may be modified in the same manner as the preceding one.

An alternative name for this design is the Cantonee Cross. While the basic symbolism is the same, an alternate meaning relates the five crosses to the five wounds of Christ. This interpretation, and the use of more restrained colors, would make this an appropriate symbol for the season of Lent.

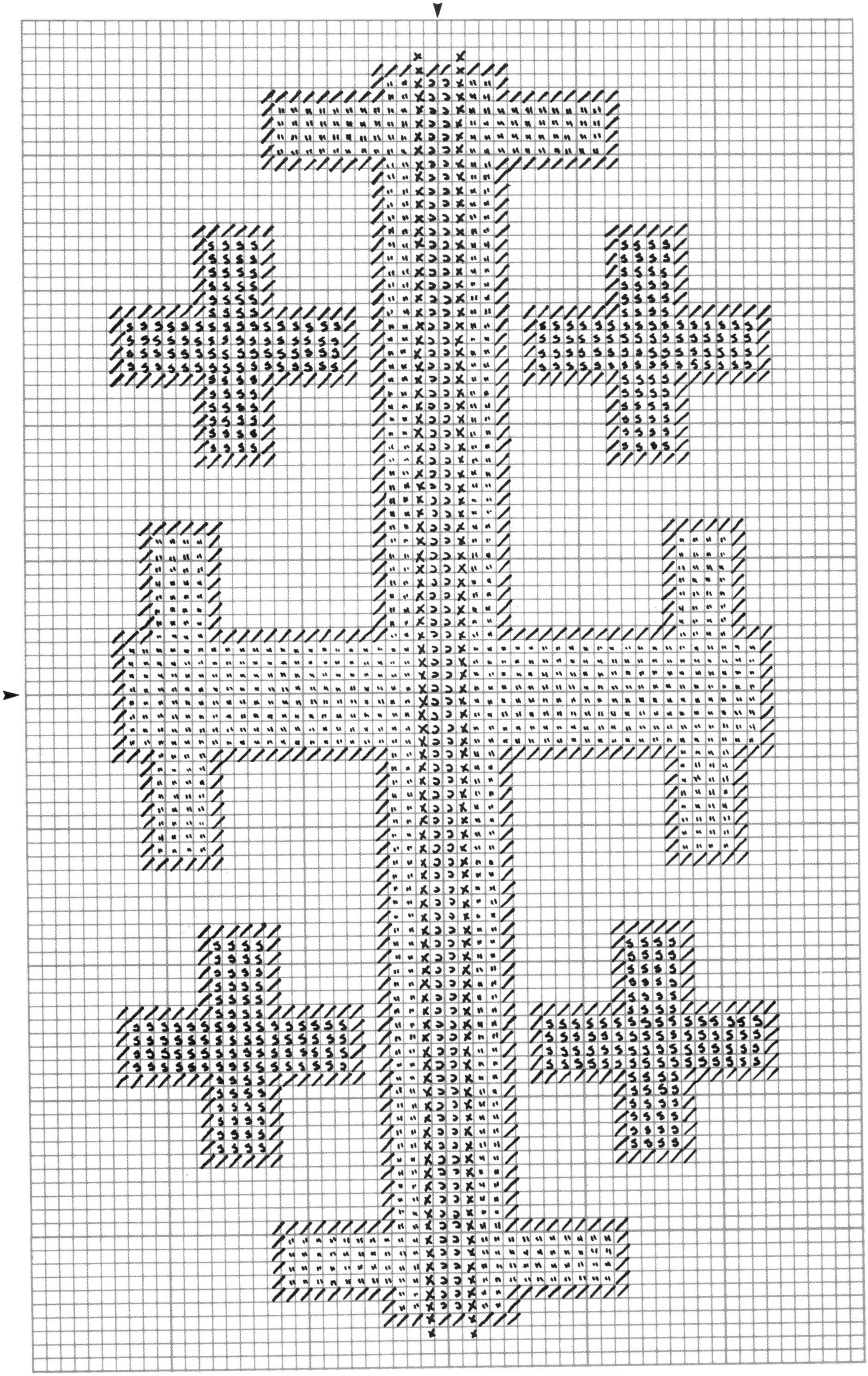

Design 9

CROSS-CROSSLET FITCHED

Suggested for use in Lent

Dimensions: 55 stitches wide by 72 stitches high

Colors:

3 = Black
X = Red

The imagery of the cross-crosslet has been examined in connection with the two previous patterns (7 and 8). This version is "fitched," or modified, by changing one of the arms into a point. The resulting symbol is appropriate for the season of Lent because the point is a reminder of the nails used to affix Jesus to the cross, while the basic symbol reminds us that even in the season of Lent we must be careful to look beyond the immediate concerns which sometimes preoccupy us to the larger mission of the Church.

If a stole which uses two different crosses is desired for the season of Lent, Design 17C is recommended. As a variation of the cross of suffering, it is appropriate for the season. In addition, that design is the same height as this design, so it will not look out of place when used with it. You will want to use the same colors for both designs, probably black and red.

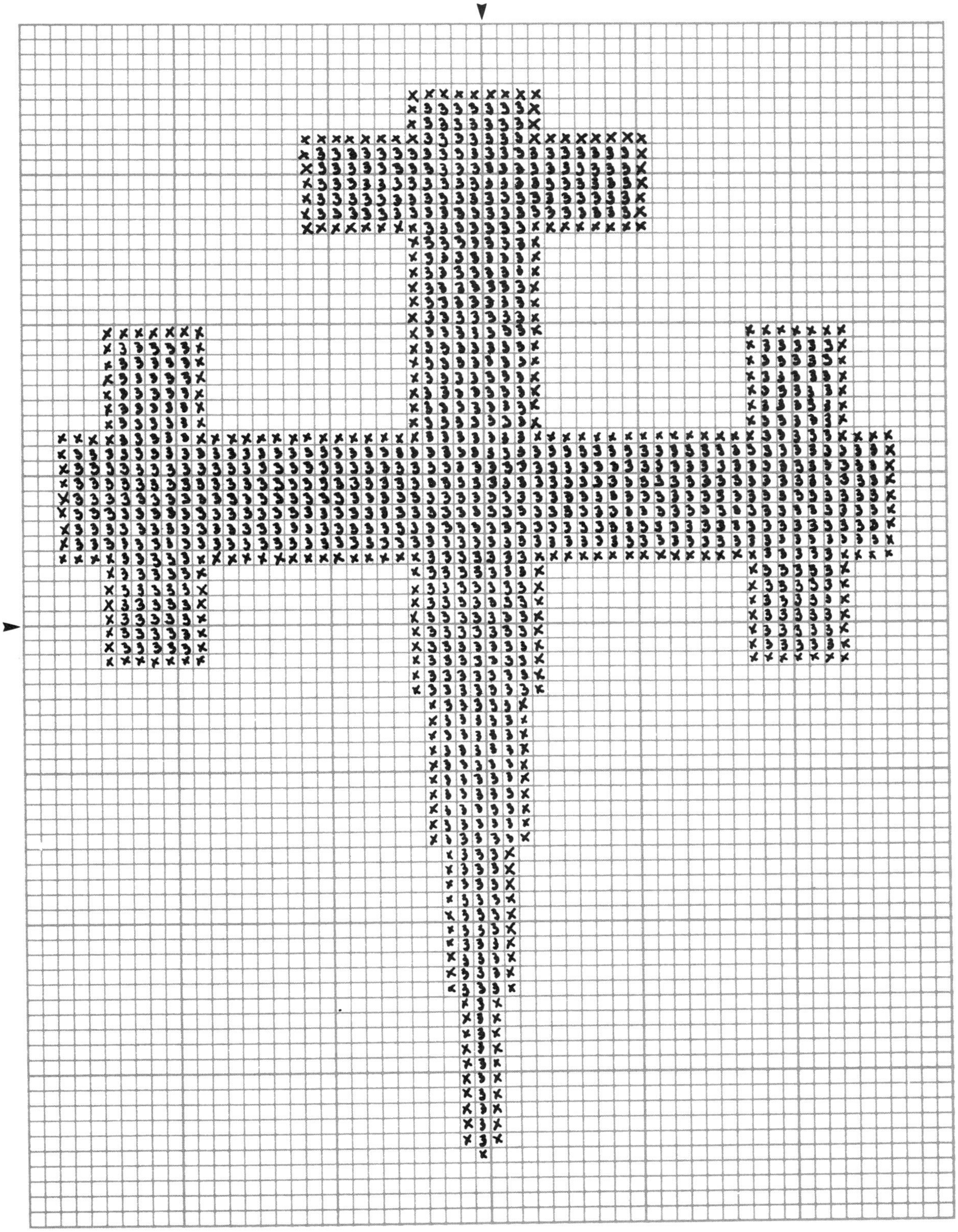

Design 10

CHALICE AND HOST

Suggested for use in Holy Week or Pentecost

Dimensions: 52 stitches wide by 105 stitches high

Colors:

/ = Gold
∝ = Silver Gray
Ɔ = White

The chalice is a part of many of the symbols attached to the various saints of the Church. Here it is used as a reminder of the events of Maundy Thursday, when Christ gave a new commandment (in Latin "mandatum," hence the name of the day) which centered around the chalice. The host or wafer emphasizes the eucharistic nature of this symbol, and the nimbus gave a sense of both the mystery of the sacrament and the manner in which its power spreads. The Baptismal shell on the chalice serves to remind us of the method by which we join the Church and the ancient tradition of baptizing newly-instructed catechumens at the conclusion of Holy Week.

This design may be modified at least two ways. First, the host and nimbus may be omitted, as by itself the chalice is a symbol of the Eucharist. Second, a cross might be substituted for the host and nimbus. Traditionally this should be a cross of suffering (see Design 17).

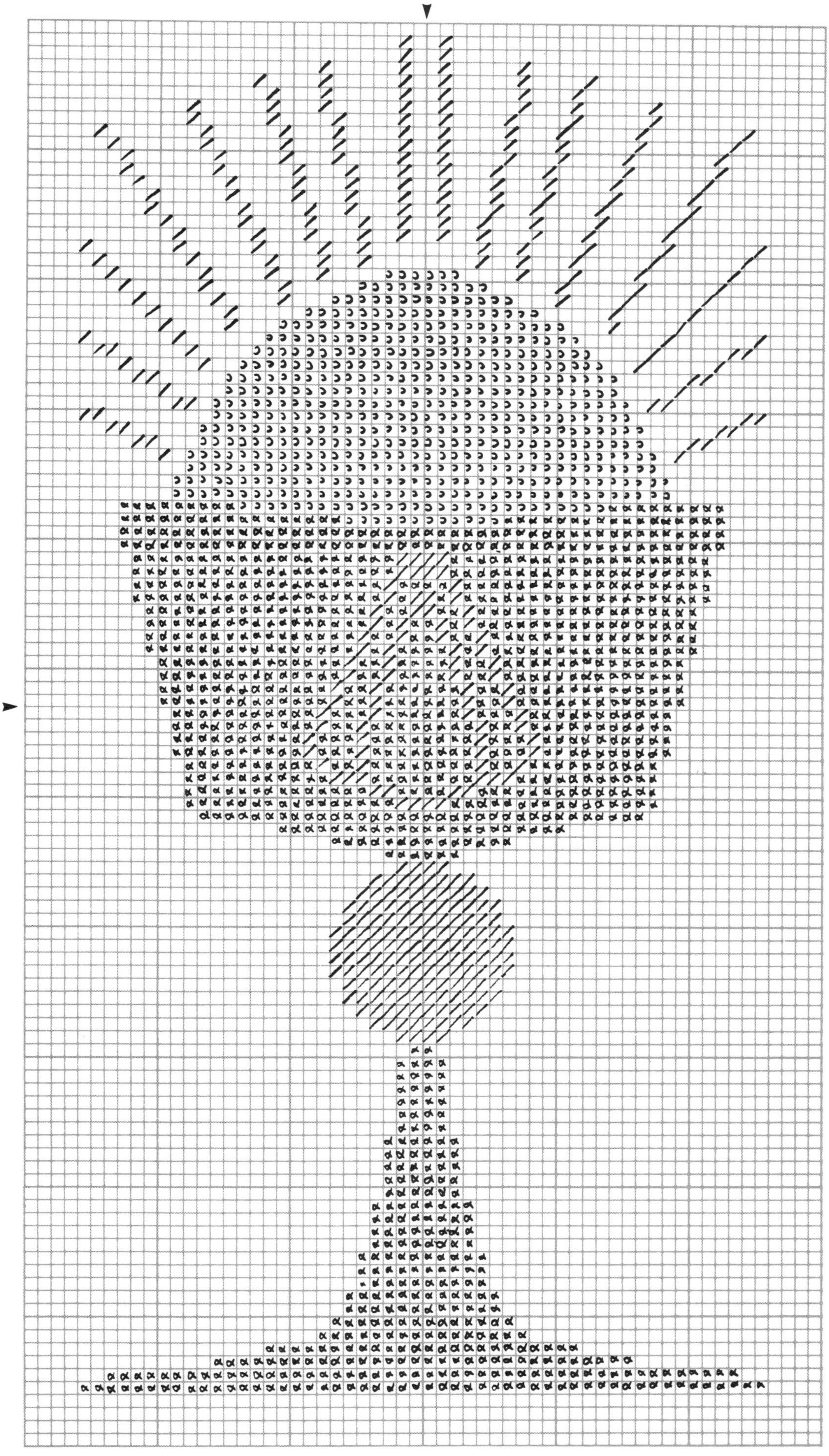

Design 11

TAU CROSS WITH CROWN OF THORNS

Suggested for use in Holy Week

Dimensions: 52 stitches wide by 105 stitches high

Colors:

    3 =   Black
    + =   Medium Brown

There is certainly no agreement about the physical shape of the cross used for the crucifixion, but some people argue that the Tau, or Egyptian, cross is a logical candidate. Together with the crown of thorns this symbol is a vivid reminder of the events of Good Friday.

Along with the preceding symbol of the chalice and host (Design 10), the stole for Holy Week includes reminders of the two major events of the week.

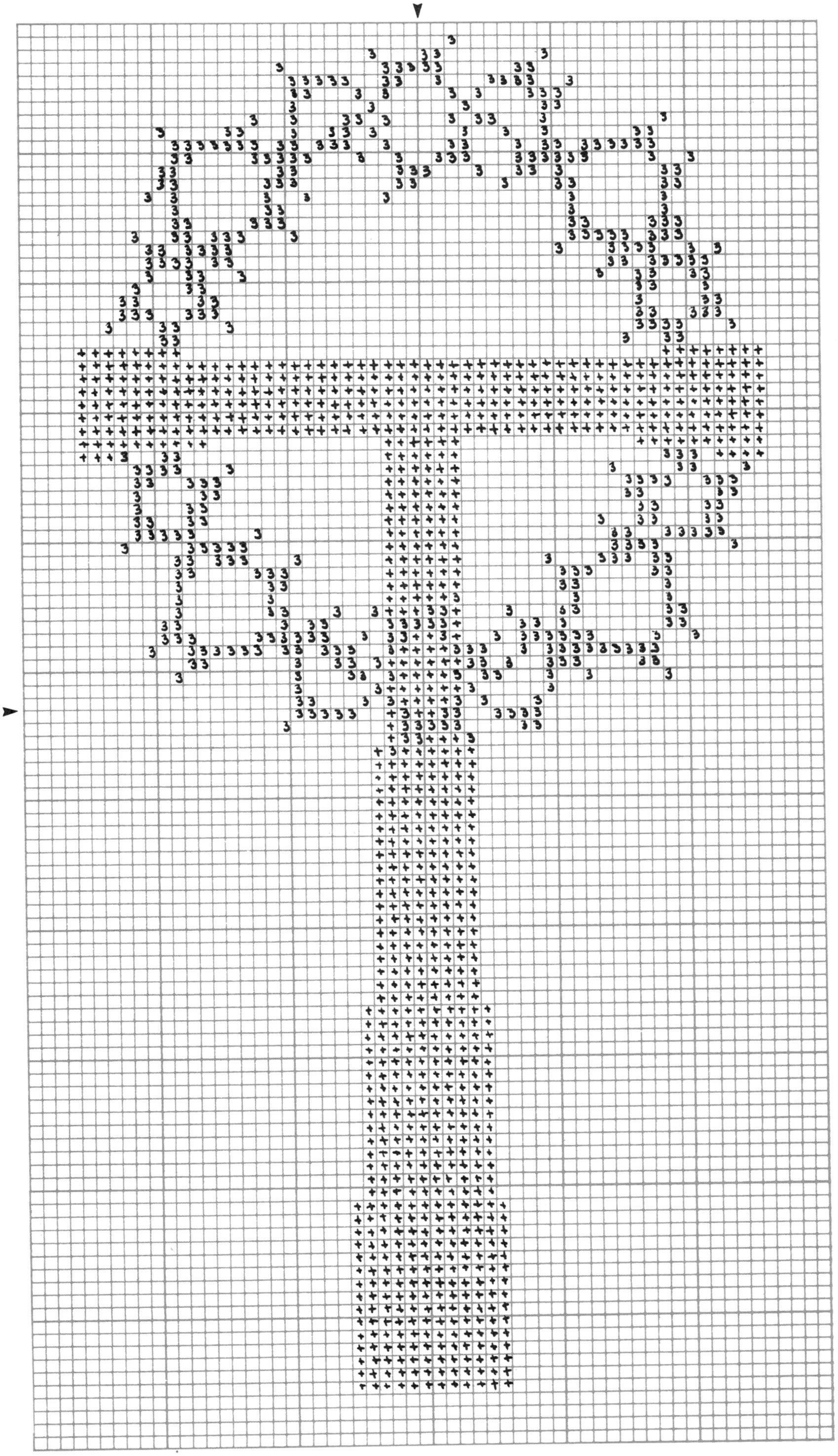

Design 12

BUTTERFLY

Suggested for use on Easter Sunday

Dimensions: 45 stitches wide by 64 stitches high

Colors:

- **3** = Black
- **=** = Light Brown
- **** = Dark Red
- **X** = Red
- **c** = Orange
- **ɔ** = White
- **ɛ** = Ecru

The butterfly is an ancient symbol of resurrection and the promise of new life in Christ. The butterfly emerging from a seemingly dead cocoon is a strong reminder of the resurrection. The life cycle of a butterfly (caterpillar, cocoon, butterfly) can be taken as a symbol of our life on earth, the grave, and new life in Christ.

The design is meant to be used with the "Alleluia" (Design 25) on the same stole. Obviously the two designs are not the same size, so an arrangement is necessary. For example, start the "Alleluia" near the shoulder of the left-hand portion of the stole (the part of the stole that will be on the left shoulder when it is worn). Place the butterfly on the bottom (leave a border) of the other side. Another alternative would use two butterflies, one on each side of the stole with no "Alleluia". In this instance it would probably be a good idea to reverse one of the butterflies so that they are facing each other.

Design 13

ANCHOR CROSS WITH CHI CROSSING

Suggested for use in Easter, Christmas, or Pentecost seasons

Dimensions: 56 stitches wide by 70 stitches high

Colors:

α = Silver Gray
X = Red

The anchor cross is an example of a common object which has been imbued with an unintended significance. Simply put, the shape of an anchor is meant to be functional, not religiously significant. Yet, because of the crossbar, the shape has taken on a symbolic meaning. The anchor cross is usually taken as a symbol of well-grounded hope, anchored in Christ. When the Greek letter "chi" (X) is added (the first letter of Christ in Greek), the symbol becomes a form of the sacred monogram and serves to remind us that grace and hope come to us through Christ. With these interpretations the symbol is appropriate for either the season of Easter or the season of Pentecost.

An alternate interpretation views the cross and "chi" as a symbol of Christ, who was born of Mary, symbolized by the crescent moon of the base. With this understanding, the symbol is also appropriate for the Christmas Season.

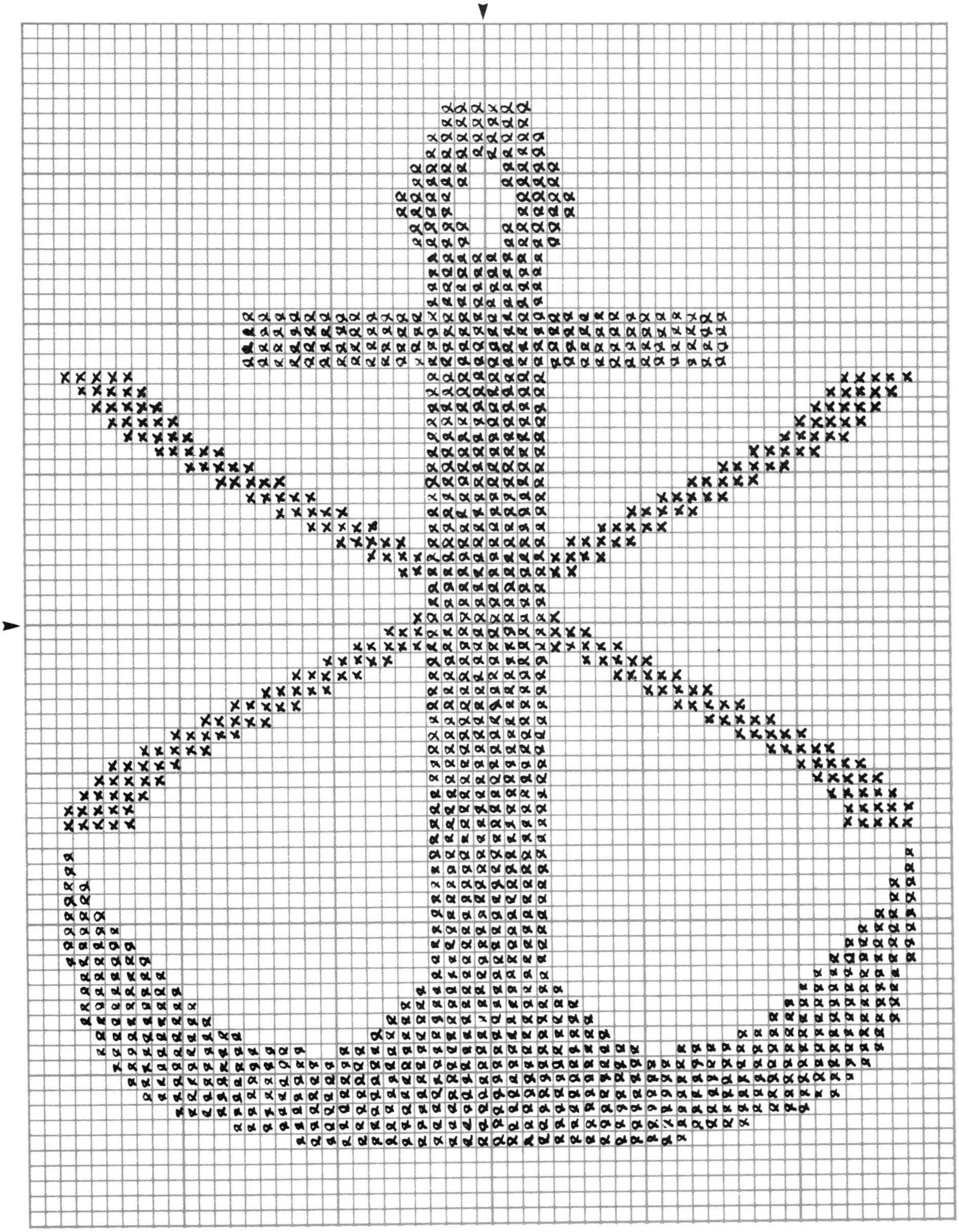

Design 14

CHI RHO AND ENCLOSURE

Suggested for use in Easter or Pentecost

Dimensions: 52 stitches wide by 72 stitches high

Colors:

    ╱ = Gold
    ✕ = Red

The basic symbol in this design is composed of the first two letters in the Greek form of the word "Christ," chi (X) and rho (P). The chi has been brought up to close over the top of the rho. The calligraphy of the Greek alphabet makes the rho appear off-center.

This is a somewhat stylized design, and it is open to at least two interpretations. The shape is somewhat reminiscent of the outline of a pomegranate, a symbol of the resurrection. As the seeds burst from the pomegranate, so too does Christ burst from the tomb. This interpretation lends itself to use during the Easter Season.

Alternatively, the general shape could also be seen as a stylized outline of a fish. The fish is an ancient symbol for Christ. The Greek word for fish is spelled with the first letters of the Greek words for "Jesus Christ, Son of God, Savior." Further, the fish is sometimes used as a symbol of the Eucharist or as a reminder of the call to be "fishers of men." These interpretations make this an appropriate symbol for the season of Pentecost.

Design 15

DESCENDING DOVE

Suggested for use on the Day of Pentecost

Dimensions: 52 stitches wide by 64 stitches high

Colors:

      ɔ =   White

      3 =   Black

The descending dove is the most familiar symbol used to represent the Holy Spirit. In Acts 2 the story of the Day of Pentecost is recounted and the gift of the Holy Spirit plays an important part in the story. It is suggested that this symbol, when used on one stole with Design 16, be placed on the upper portion of the side of the stole that hangs over the left shoulder.

    Greek does not distinguish between doves and pigeons (whose other common name is rock dove). Usually translators will opt for the word "dove" as a more suitable choice, but linguistically, the image could also be that of a pigeon. The dove (or pigeon) is often represented with a three-rayed nimbus signifying that the Spirit is a member of the Trinity.

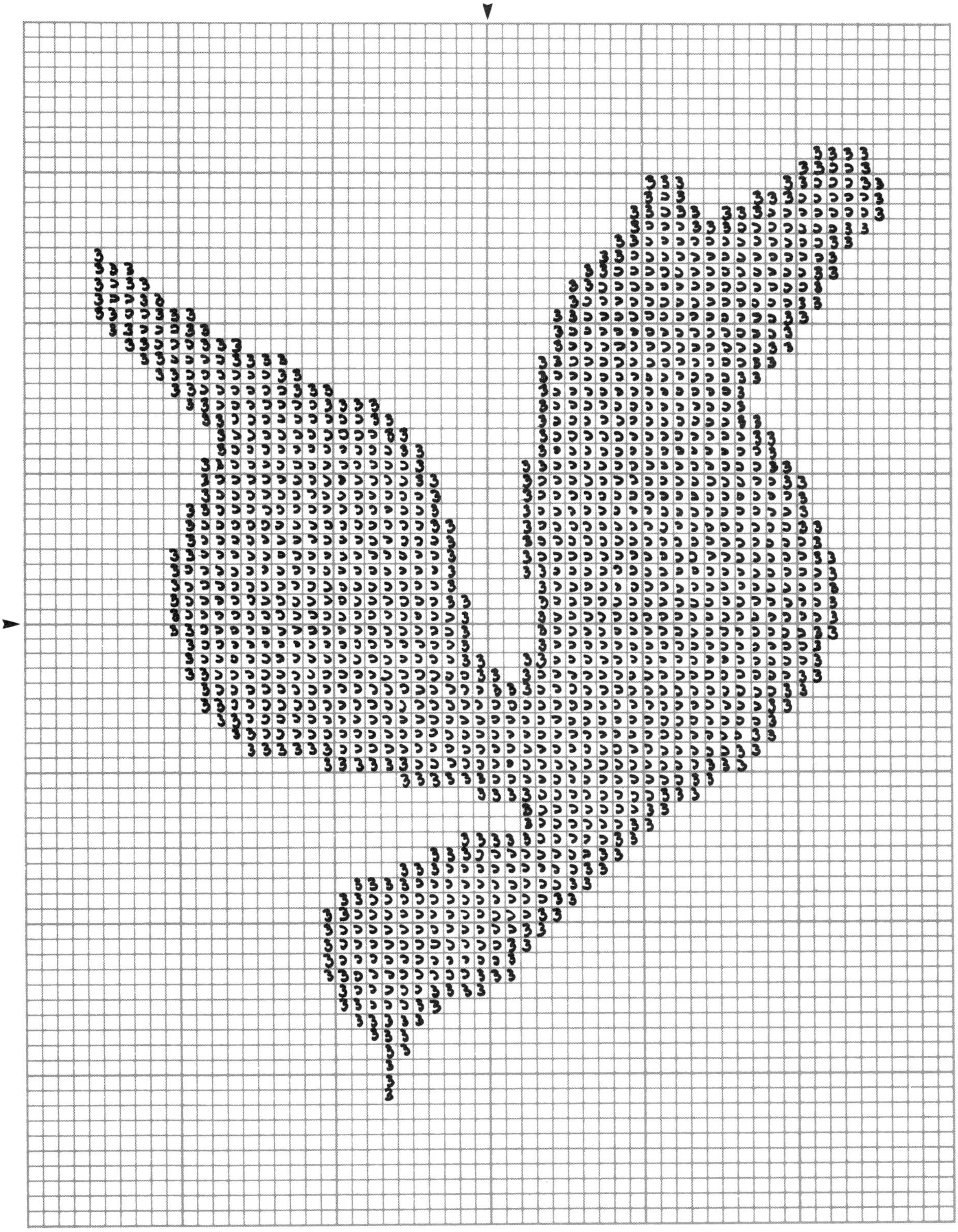

Design 16

FLAMES AND SILHOUETTES

Suggested for use on the Day of Pentecost

Dimensions: 52 stitches wide by 98 stitches high

Colors:

- ╱ = Gold
- ╲ = Dark Red
- ✗ = Red
- ∧ = Pink
- ⊂ = Orange
- ϡ = Black

This design is meant to be a symbolic representation of the events of the Day of Pentecost as recounted in Acts 2. Originally Pentecost was not a Christian festival; rather, it began as a Jewish festival that gained a particularly Christian significance because of the events that took place during the Pentecost festival immediately after the resurrection.

When used with Design 15 on a single stole, this design should probably be placed near the bottom of the portion of the stole that hangs over the right shoulder.

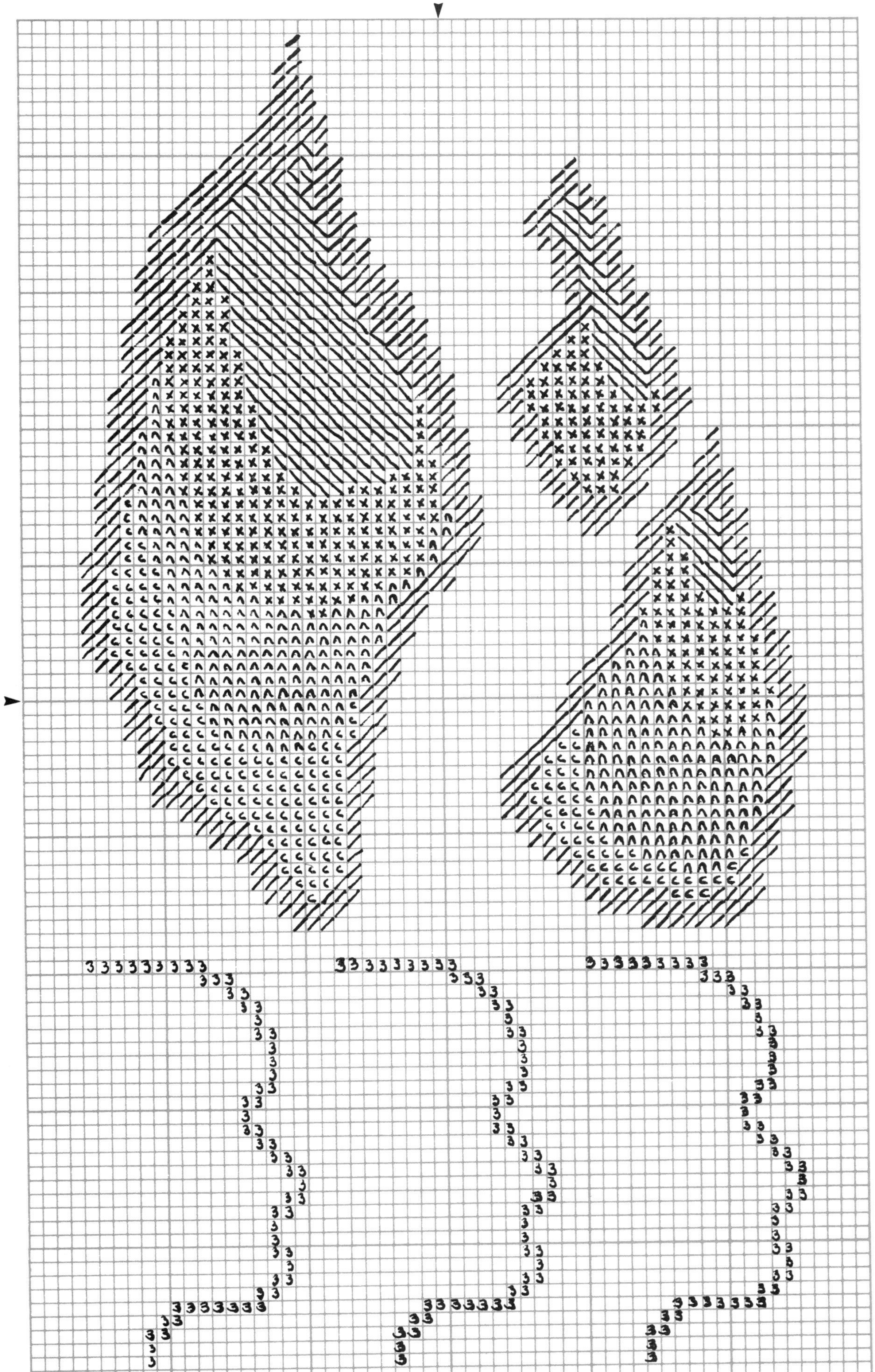

Designs 17A, 17B, and 17C

CROSS OF SUFFERING, ENTRAILED

Suggested for use in Pentecost, or any other Season

Dimensions: (17A) 54 stitches wide by 54 stitches high
(17B) 54 stitches wide by 67 stitches high
(17C) 48 stitches wide by 72 stitches high

Colors:

/ = Gold
6 = Light Blue
⟋ = Light Blue Half Stitch

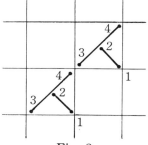

Fig. 8

First, a note about the new stitch that is introduced for this design. A half stitch is exactly what the name implies. The method to use to make the stitch is shown in Figure 8. One of the ideas of this book has been to make everything as simple as possible so that people who are not familiar with counted cross stitch would not have to figure out highly complicated directions. In this instance, it is necessary to introduce this new stitch to give the arms of the cross the proper pointed appearance.

The cross itself, with the pointed ends, is sometimes called the Cross of Suffering. The basic design (17A) is also a Greek cross (since all the arms are of equal length). This is probably the simplest design in the book and relatively easy to execute. You should purchase two skeins of the color you are going to use for the cross and one skein of the color for the decoration around it for each design on a stole.

Following the basic design are two variations to give you an idea of some of the possibilities that exist. Design 17B has been changed from a Greek to a Latin cross (one of the arms has been extended.) Design 17C has been changed in two ways. It has been extended both up and down and the entire design has been narrowed by six stitches. You can, of course, continue to modify the basic design to suit your own tastes. The colors can be changed as well as the shape.

It is also possible to use the central portion of this design (the part marked in Light Blue on the chart) to modify Design 10. In the event that you are interested, the process works like this. Eliminate the Host and Nimbus from Design 10, then add the Cross of Suffering (Design 17A) to the center of the top of the chalice. The best way to add the Cross of Suffering is to drop the point on the bottom and begin with the first complete row of stitches. You might want to change the color to the more somber black for this use.

If you desire a set of stoles with identical patterns on each stole, this design is suggested for the project. It has the advantage of being simple to work, and if desired, some variation can be accomplished with different colors for the design.

Continuous lines at points of Cross denote the half stitch.

Continuous lines at points of Cross denote the half stitch.

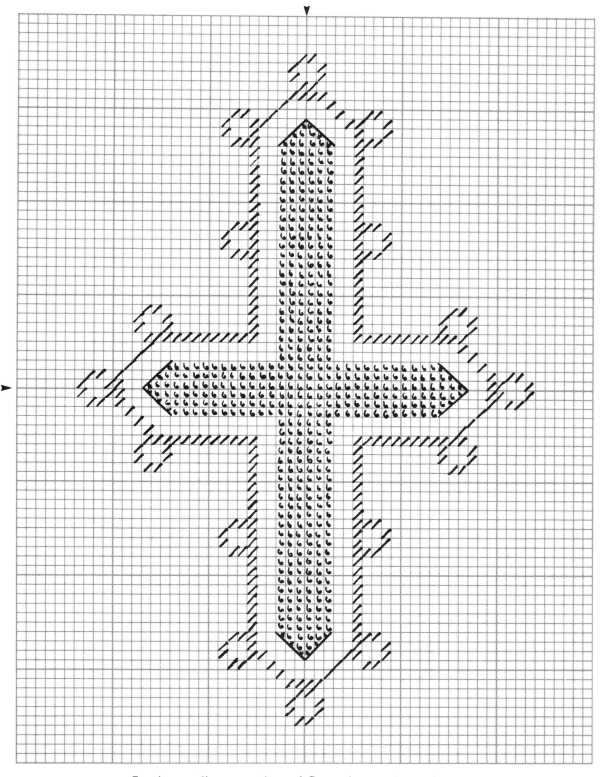

Continuous lines at points of Cross denote the half stitch.

Design 18

GRADED (CALVARY) CROSS WITH WHEAT AND GRAPES

Suggested for use in Pentecost Season

Dimensions: 43 stitches wide by 97 stitches high

Colors:

    ╱ =   Gold
    + =   Medium Brown
    β =   Light Yellow
    ∧ =   Dark Green
    o =   Green
    y =   Light Green
    ▲ =   Purple

The Cross used in this design is intended to be reminiscent of the style of cross used in many churches. If desired, the design may be modified by omitting the base and using only the Latin cross which remains. The wheat and grapes are a reminder of the Eucharist, the sacrament for strengthening Christians, a fitting symbol for the Pentecost Season. The three leaves can be seen as either a reminder of the Holy Trinity or, because of the colors used, as a reminder of the growth in grace of individual members.

Design 19

ANCHOR CROSS, CHI RHO, AND ALPHA AND OMEGA

Suggested for use on Saints' Days (Red), Easter, or Pentecost

Dimensions: 50 stitches wide by 70 stitches high

Color:

/ = Gold

Ideally, perhaps, it would be nice to have a special stole for each day when a saint is remembered with a symbol for that saint on the stole. Such a production is beyond the scope of this book. Instead, there are four designs (19, 20, 21, 22,) which may be used on red or white stoles. These two colors are the colors usually assigned for such days. These symbols may also be used for seasonal stoles.

The Anchor Cross and the Chi Rho monogram have been discussed in connection with other designs. This variation of the Anchor Cross is not as appropriate for use during the Christmas Season because the flukes of the anchor are not arranged in the half moon form that is suggestive of Mary. The Alpha and Omega are a reference to the description of Jesus in Revelation 1:17, with the first (Alpha—A—is the first letter of the Greek alphabet) and the last (Omega—Ω—is the last letter) symbolically presented. This design is based on an emblem found in the catacombs, which makes the design especially appropriate for Saints' Days which use the color red since red is the color suggestive of martyrdom.

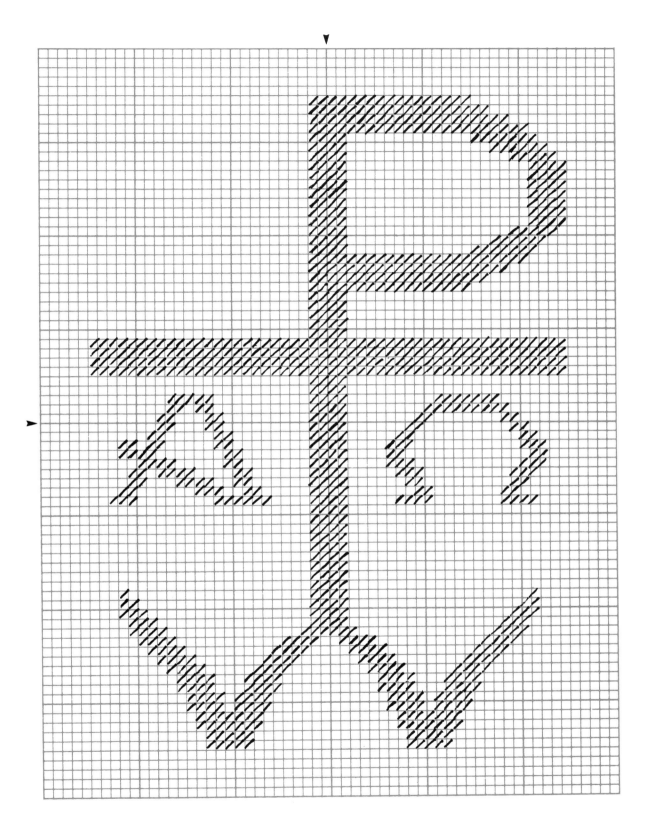

Design 20

SHIP

Suggested for use on Saints' Days (Red) or during the Pentecost Season

Dimensions: 50 stitches wide by 70 stitches high

Colors:

+ = Medium Brown

= = Light Brown

The ship is one of the older symbols used to represent the Church. The mast reminds us of the importance of Christ and the Cross in our journey. It could also be pointed out that the Church, like a ship, carries the faithful through the storms of this life. The image also brings to mind the various incidents involving ships in Christ's life.

The three divisions on the side of the ship, as with most uses of three in Christian symbolism, are a reminder of the Trinity.

The symbol of a ship finds a further expression in our word for the central portion of a church, the "nave," which comes from the Latin word for ship. Many Danish Lutheran congregations have models of ships suspended from the ceiling as reminders of this symbolic meaning as well as a reminder of the members of the congregation who follow nautical livelihoods.

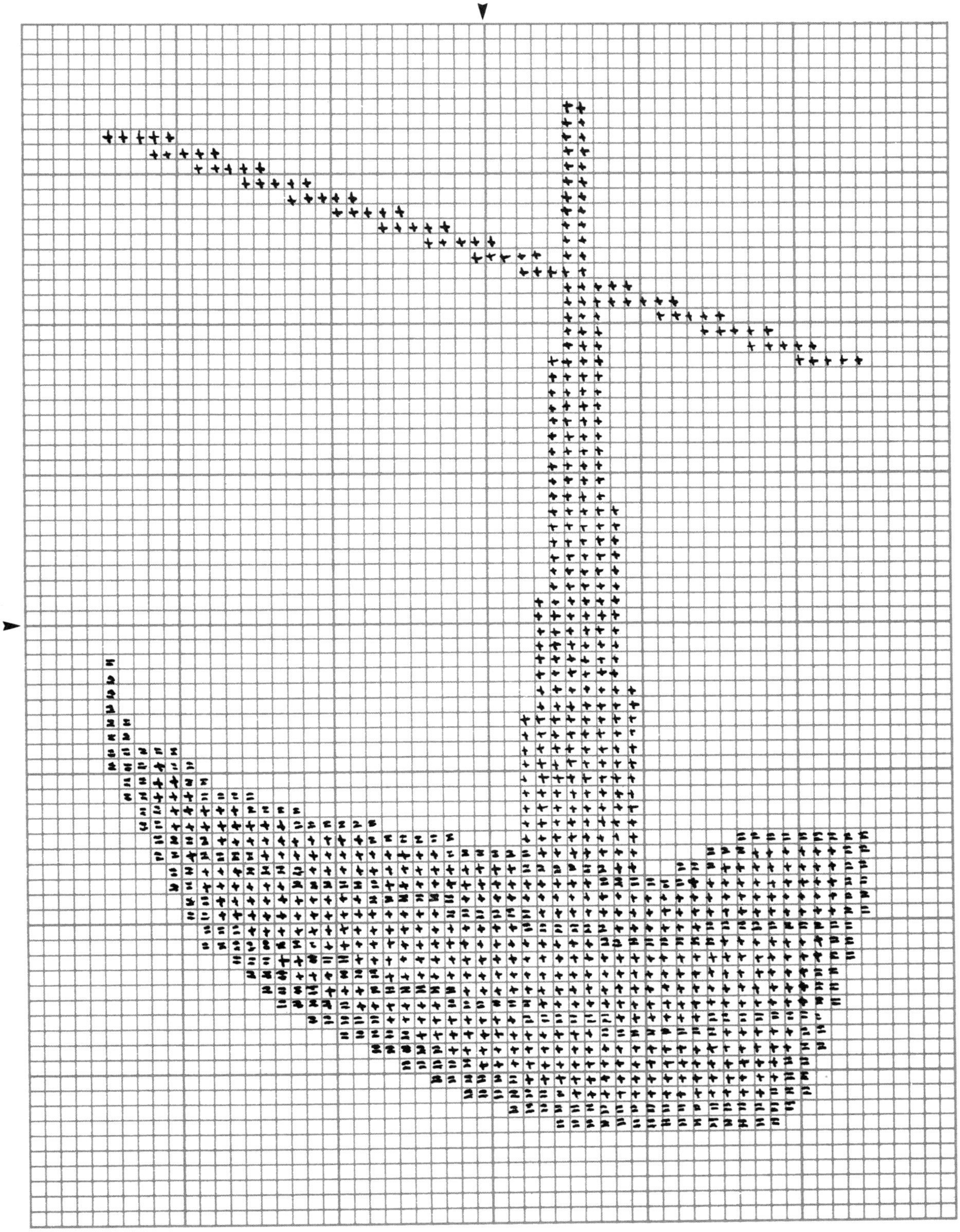

Design 21

INTERLOCKING CIRCLES

Suggested for use on Trinity Sunday, Saints' Days (White), or during the Pentecost Season

Dimensions: 50 stitches wide by 50 stitches high

Color:

∕ = Gold

The three interlocking circles of this symbol form a classic symbol that represents the Holy Trinity in both the unity and diversity which is found in this doctrine. The intersection of the circles forms another symbol of the Trinity, an equilateral triangle, which emphasizes the equality of the members of the Trinity.

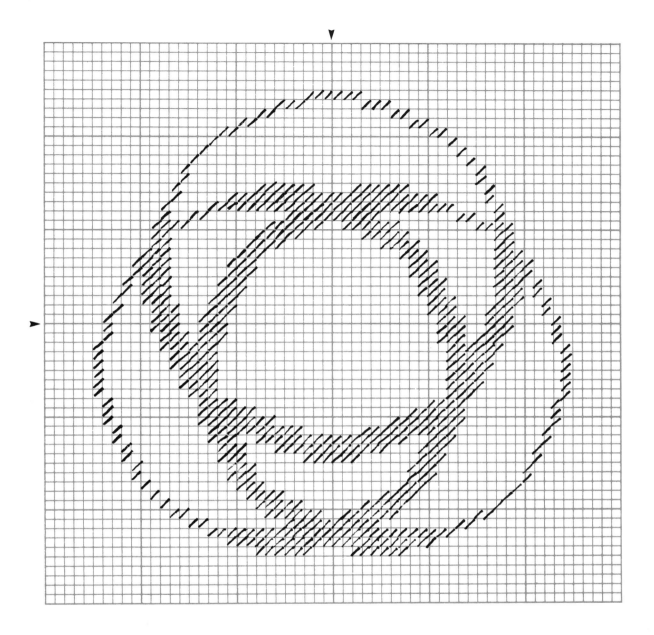

Design 22

CELTIC CROSS, CHALICE, AND HOST

Suggested for use with any color

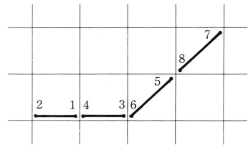

Dimensions: 60 stitches wide by 62 stitches high

Colors:

    c = Orange
    ⌣ = Backstitch in Orange (Two strands recommended)   Fig. 9

This pattern is the only pattern which uses only one strand of floss. In other words, separate one strand from the six strands that are normally used, and use that one strand only. Any color of floss can be used for this design, but bright, contrasting colors work best. Because of the nature of the design, even the brightest colors will be somewhat muted by the color of the fabric which shows through the stitches.

This style of work is called Assisi embroidery after the village in Italy where it was developed. The real design is found in those portions of the fabric which are not covered with floss. The cross used here is a Celtic cross, a symbol of eternal salvation, an aspect of the Eucharist which is highlighted by the inclusion of the Chalice and the Host.

One modification of this design would be to use a metallic (both gold and silver are commonly available) floss. On a darker stole the result should be striking, but also fairly expensive.

Design 23

CROSS, BAPTISMAL SHELL, CHALICE, AND HOST

Suggested for use with any color

Dimensions: 60 stitches wide by 32 stitches high

Colors:

/ = Gold
β = Light Yellow
= = Light Brown
✗ = Red
∩ = Pink
ᕹ = Light Blue
ᒡ = Silver Gray
ᒑ = White

This design and the preceding one (22) are both forms of something called orphrey bandings. These designs may be used on any color stole and the finished product looks relatively plain and simple.

Orphrey bandings were first used on chasubles to hide the seams which were necessary because of the inability of the looms of that time to produce material wide enough for a chasuble. In time the orphrey bandings grew wider and more decorative. Today, even though they are no longer needed to cover the seams (which are often not there, anyway), orphrey bandings are still used as simple decorations for both stoles and chasubles.

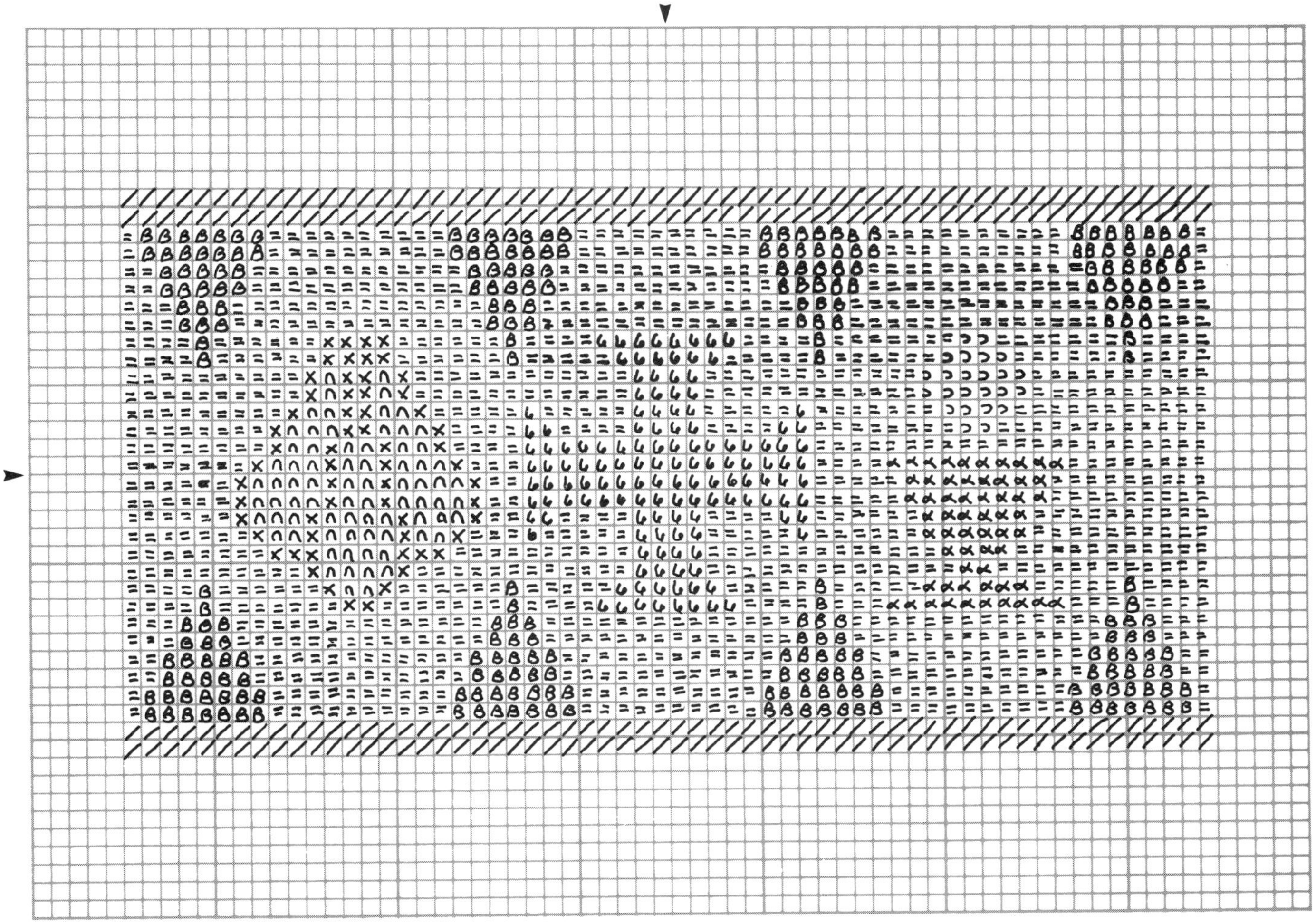

Design 24

SEVEN LAMPS

Suggested for use on Saints' Days (White) or during the Pentecost Season

Dimensions: 49 stitches wide by 203 stitches high

Colors:

      ╱ = Gold
      3 = Black
      ╲ = Dark Red
      ✗ = Red

The use of seven objects is significant in itself. Seven is thought to be the number of completion or perfection. Seven candles or flames or lights may be taken to represent the seven gifts of the Holy Spirit: Wisdom, Understanding, Counsel, Moral Might, Knowledge, Godliness, and the Fear of the Lord. Further, seven lamps can also be interpreted as a sign of the seven churches of Revelation 2-3.

    If desired, a single lamp can be used as a design. If this choice is selected, a single lamp could be taken as a representation of the Sanctuary Lamp which reminds us of the eternal presence of God in Christ among us.

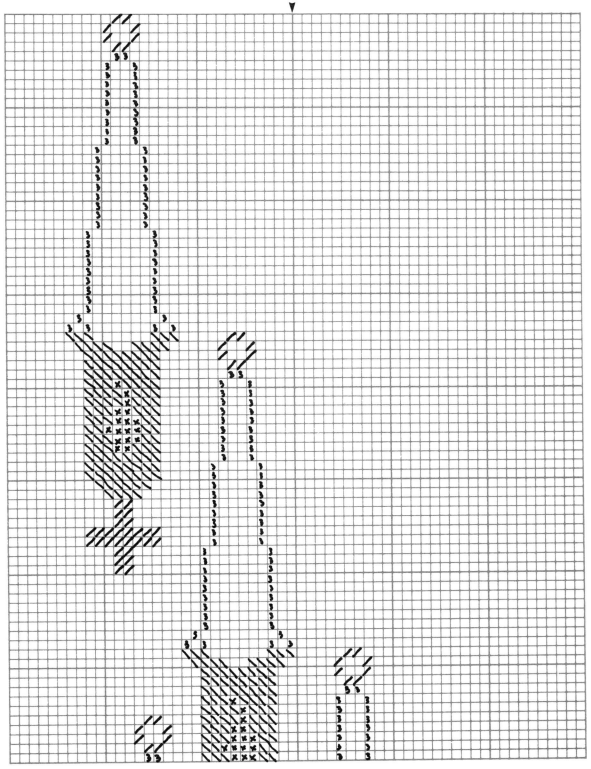

Pattern continues

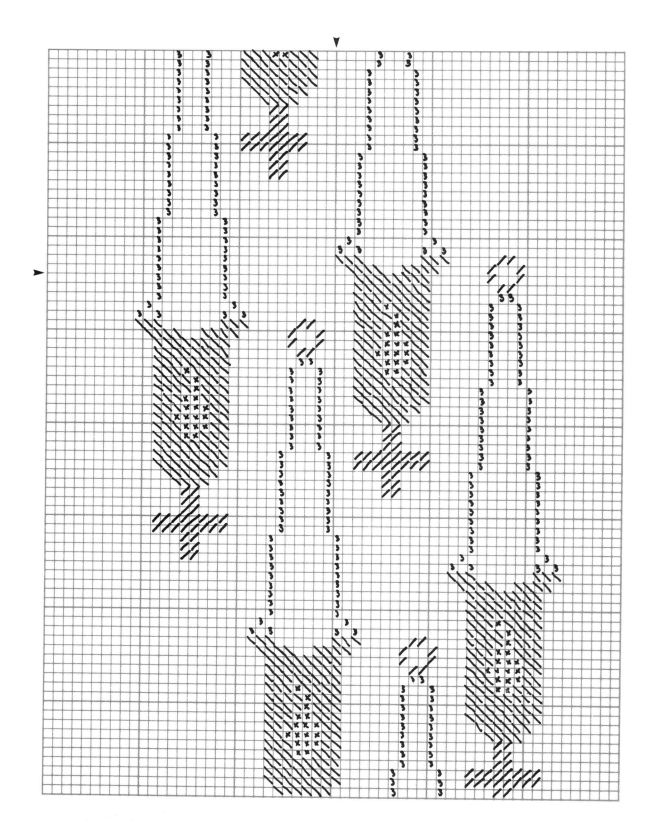

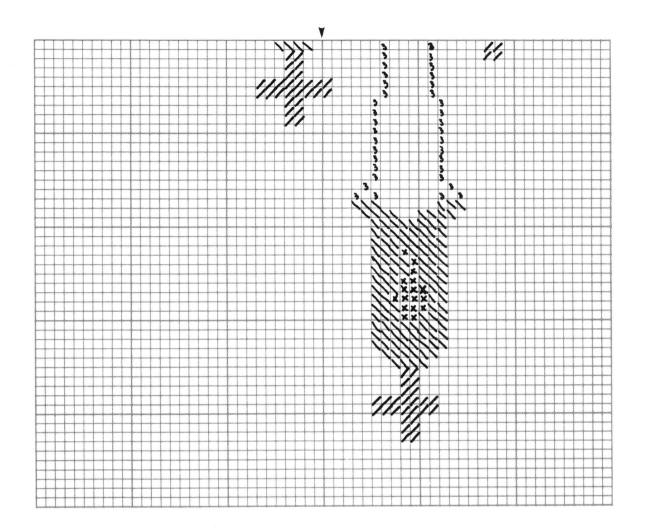

Design 25

ALLELUIA

Suggested for use on Easter Sunday

Dimensions: 54 stitches wide by 330 stitches high

Color:

X = Red

The word "Alleluia" comes from the Greek form of a Hebrew word which means "Praise to Yahweh," or "Praise the Lord." The word appears occasionally in the Psalms, where it appears to have served as either a call to worship or perhaps as a liturgical response to the Psalm. It is understood to be an expression of both joy and praise. In the New Testament the word appears only in the book of Revelation, and only in Chapter 19. In these places the word also seems to have some liturgical significance which is consistent with the way it was used in the Old Testament.

"Alleluia" has become closely associated with the celebration of Easter, perhaps because it appears in so many of the hymns used on that day and during the season of Easter. As a call of joy and praise to God, this word is certainly an appropriate symbol for Easter.

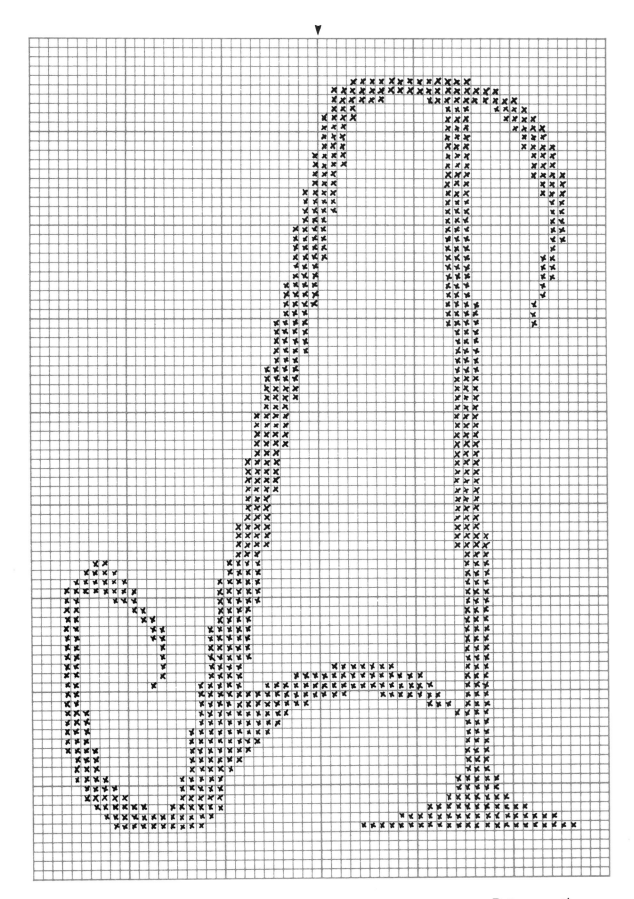

5 lines to top of "L"

Pattern continues

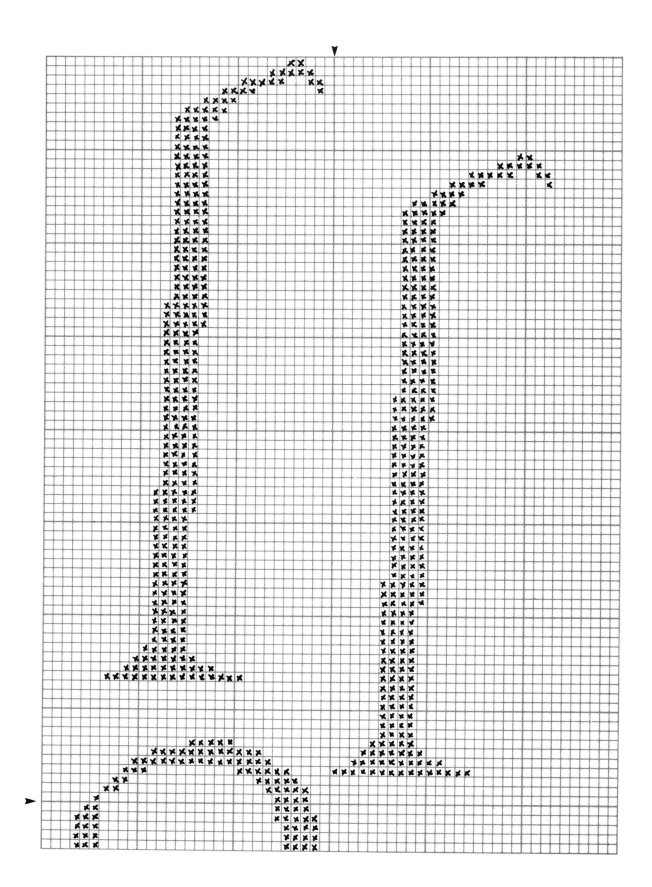

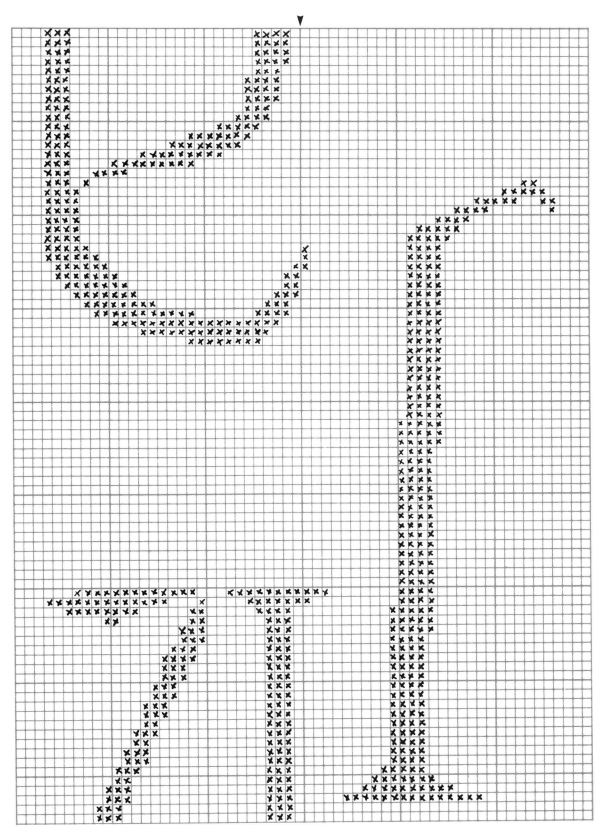

Pattern continues

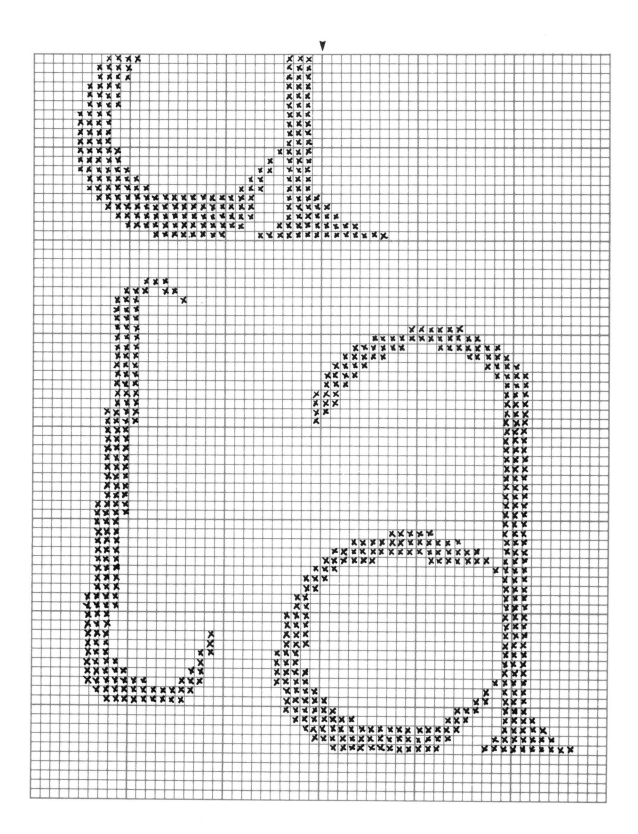

INDEX OF COLORS

Color	Design	1	2	3	4	5	6	7	8	9	10	11	12	13	14	15	16	17	18	19	20	21	22	23	24	25
Gold	/	X	X	X	X	X	X	X	X		X				X		X	X	X	X		X		X	X	
Red	✗	X	X		X			X	X	X			X	X	X		X							X	X	X
Black	ろ			X	X	X	X			X		X	X			X	X								X	
Flesh	J		X																							
White	ↄ			X	X	X		X	X		X		X			X								X		
Light Blue	6			X	X	X	X											X						X		
Medium Brown	+				X							X							X		X					
Turquoise	⌇							X	X																	
Pale Green	‖							X	X																	
Orange	c												X				X						X			
Dark Red	＼												X				X								X	
Light Brown	=												X								X			X		
Silver Gray	α										X			X										X		
Pink	∩																	X						X		
Light Yellow	β																			X				X		
Ecru	ε												X													
Dark Green	∧																		X							
Green	o																		X							
Light Green	Y																		X							
Purple	▲																		X							

   The purpose of this index is to help guide you in purchasing floss. For example, the colors of flesh and ecru are used in only one design each, so a single skein of each color should suffice. (These are also the only two colors which might be difficult to find at a discount store.) Gold, on the other hand, is used in so many designs that you can safely buy that extra skein or two when planning a stole with expectations of using it eventually.

INDEX OF SEASONAL SUGGESTED USES

Design number	Dimensions (width x height in stitches)	Advent	Christmas	Epiphany	Lent	Holy Week	Easter	Pentecost	Saints' Days
1	54 x 70	X					X		
2	52 x 70	X		S				S	
3	56 x 56		X						
4	56 x 56		X						
5	55 x 55			D					
6	56 x 56			D					
7	48 x 94			S				S	
8	48 x 94			S	X			S	
9	55 x 72				X				
10	52 x 105					X		X	
11	52 x 105					X			
12	45 x 64						X		
13	56 x 70		X				S	S	
14	52 x 72						S	S	
15	52 x 64							D	
16	52 x 98							D	
17A	54 x 54	X	X	X	X	X	X	X	
17B	54 x 67	X	X	X	X	X	X	X	
17C	48 x 72	X	X	X	X	X	X	X	
18	43 x 97							S	
19	50 x 70						S	S	X (Red)
20	50 x 70							S	X (Red)
21	50 x 50							S	X (White, (Trinity Sunday)
22	60 x 62	X	X	X	X	X	X	X	
23	60 x 32	X	X	X	X	X	X	X	
24	49 x 203							S	X (White)
25	54 x 330						D		

D = The Day of
S = Season
X = Both Day and Season